Presented to
Bridport Central
School – Grade 4
from the
Bridport Bicentennial
Committee 1989

Students who participated in logo contest:

1 Bobby Jackman
2 Becca Barrett
3 Melinda Piper
4 Corey Torrey
5 Jana McQueeney
6 Jonathan Huestis
7 Jason Mereier

VERMONT
a special world

Glover Porch, by Mack Derick

RALPH N. HILL/MURRAY HOYT/WALTER R. HARD, JR.

VERMONT

a special world

VERMONT LIFE MAGAZINE   MONTPELIER, VERMONT

ISBN: 0-936896-02-7

Published by *Vermont Life* Magazine, Montpelier, Vermont.
Distributed to bookstores outside of Vermont by
Houghton Mifflin Company, Boston, Massachusetts.

Seventh Edition 1983
Sixth Edition 1979
Fifth Edition 1976
Fourth Edition 1973
Third Edition 1971
Second Edition 1969

Library of Congress Catalog Card Number 68-29894

Front cover picture: Barnet, by Winston Pote
Back cover picture: Woodstock, by Abner Kodess

Designed by Linda Dean Paradee

Manufactured in the United States of America

Contents

We have met here to dedicate and consecrate this extensive wilderness and give it a new name, which new name is Verd-Mont in token that her mountains and hills shall be ever green and shall never die.

— The Reverend Samuel Peters
October, 1768

That the Green Mountain land, and her people, too, embody qualities that are subtly yet definitely different from other states', has been constantly remarked upon by almost two centuries of visitors to this region. In the past fifty years, especially, Vermont has become a casebook situation of America in microcosm, meeting with varying degrees of success the great forces of change to life and land.

Vermont's topography, and especially its climate and its extremes of seasonal demarcation, create a combination of breathtaking beauty with harsh austerity, which has been transmuted to the character of Vermonters themselves. The bitter-sweet traits of the traditional Vermonters have moderated under growing contact with the wider world to where they have become less noticeably different from other Americans' than they once were. But still Vermonters are imbued with a strong feeling of heritage and tradition, and with the physical presence of the land they live in.

For those who visit, Vermont's most evident distinctions are her green-clad mountains, the white clustered villages, the winding valley roads and the hill-girt lakes. Just as travelers have been reporting their impressions of this land more than of the people, so this book's interpretation is strongly visual. It is the most extensive color pictorial record of Vermont ever published.

The writings which accompany these pictorial impressions follow the seasons also, and in the triad arrangement in each season the editors also span the many years of Vermont's recorded past. In much the same time sequence the photographic arrangements in each season tend to present an historical sweep beginning with scenes of the natural landscape and progressing to scenes of life today.

The writings in this book have been selected by two of *Vermont Life* Magazine's Senior Editors, Ralph Nading Hill and Murray Hoyt, and by the Magazine's Managing Editor, Walter Hard, Jr.

Through the years Vermont has established in many people a feeling of uniqueness, yet in a way that allows manifold individual interpretations. Thus Mr. Hill has delineated the Vermont of its early days directly in the words, (at times taken from longer passages and altered for easier modern reading), of a variety of explorers, intrepid travelers, missionaries and bold pioneers.

The center period of time, particularly around the turn of the century, Mr. Hoyt treats with in four seasonal essays, told in a personal and often a humorous vein, about the way of life that was dominant here such a short time ago, which is now greatly changed as most people know it, but which still is valid in many Vermonters' minds.

The final essays in the seasonal triads discuss, in the words of many intimate observers, the pressures for change which have come to Vermont so strongly in the past forty years. These are changes which first influenced Vermont's older social and economic life, and then, more recently, have affected the physical environment itself. Essays by four other writers illuminate in specific terms the marked and sometimes humorous changes which have developed in the last few years.

spring

Sugaring, Pleasant Valley,
by Clyde Smith

Apple Blossoms, Cornwall, by VDD

East Corinth, by Hans Wendler

Spring Run-off, by Hanson Carroll

Sugaring near Wilmington,
by John Harris

Sugaring, Jeffersonville, by Grant Heilman

White Tail at Bolton, by Bullaty-Lomeo

Mt. Mansfield from Jeffersonville, by Grant Heilman

Howe Bridge, Tunbridge, by John H. Vondell

Red Maple Buds, by Ernest Gay

14 /

All to the Borders

RALPH N. HILL

All the towns upon the lake Champlain and for three teer back the best sort of land. Not very heavy timbered, or stony or mountainous, well intersected with streams, and the streams full of small fish. Moose plenty on the mountains over against Jericho, Essex and Colchester. People hunt them in lieu of beef and get their tallow. Bears and wolves plenty. Beach, maple, pine, hemlock, cherry, birch and some oak and walnut. About 40 families in a town, about 40 towns totally unsettled. Land extraordinarily good from Rutland and Tinmouth clear to Canada line.

All sadly parsimonious, many profane, yet cheerful and much more contented than in Hartford [Connecticut], and the women more contented than the men, turned tawney by the smoke of the log-huts. Dress coarse and mean and nasty and ragged. Some very clever women and men, serious and sensible. Scarcely any sensible preaching. They were charmed with my sermons and my delivery and bestowed encomiums which it would be vain in me to repeat, such as the very first rate, philosophical, deep, penetrating, a great Scholar, angelic.

When I go from hut to hut, from town to town in the Wilderness, the people nothing to eat, to drink or wear, all work, and yet the women quiet, serene, peaceable, contented, loving their husbands, their home, wanting never to return, nor any dressy clothes; I think how strange! I ask myself are these women of the same species with our fine Ladies? Tough are they, brawney their limbs, their young girls unpolished and will bear work as well as mules. Woods make people love one another and kind and obliging and good natured. They set much more by one another than in the old settlements. Leave their doors unbarred. Sleep quietly amid flees, bedbugs, dirt and rags. O how vile, how guilty, how ungrateful to providence are our women! Tell lies about one another, envy one another, go abroad, dress and enjoy fine roads, carriages, husbands to wait on them, and are yet uneasy, unaffectionate!

I grieve to hear what thousands and thousands have endured in coming to this State of Vermont. One thing is now deeply affecting. The frowns of the Almighty are on this State for their sins. A famine is now felt in this land. Several women I saw had lived four or five days without any food, and had eight or ten Children starving around them, crying for bread and the poor women had wept till they looked like Ghosts.

I perform this day the office of physician and nurse to Mrs. Chittenden, who is very sick with a disorder called St. Anthony's fire. They seem to love me as a brother, and the Governor as a son. I struck them upon the right key. Queer is human nature and has a blind side. His Excellency picked me out to understand human nature at first sight.

About one quarter of the inhabitants and almost all the men of learning deists in the State. People pay little regard to the Sabbath, hunt and fish on that day. Not more than 1/6 part of the families attend family prayer in the whole State. About 1/2 would be glad to have the Gospel. The rest would chuse to have no Sabbath, no ministers, no religion, no heaven, no hell, no morality.

— Nathan Perkins, 1789

Country Home, Williamsville, by John H. Vondell

Fishing the Battenkill, by Hanson Carroll

East Corinth, by Hans Wendler

28 /

Opening Day Ritual

MURRAY HOYT

There are Vermonters to whom, quite simply, Spring means trout fishing. To these fine, dedicated individuals Opening Day is sacrosanct. They train their wives early that unimportant matters like jobs, responsibilities, relatives, anniversaries and the like must never be allowed to interfere with the reverent solemnization of this annual event.

The spring after my marriage in the early nineteen-thirties I inaugurated such a wife-training program. For the site of my Opening Day operations I chose the East Middlebury River, at the foot of the Green Mountains.

The only drawback was that Marg, my wife, needed the car. However, a good resourceful trout fisherman who has made up his mind to go fishing is seldom stymied by so trivial a matter as this. We decided that Marg would drive me over to the stream and then go about her business. Late in the day she would return and pick me up.

We rose while it was still dark and unbelievably cold. We ate breakfast, made me a couple of sandwiches, and started out. I wanted to be on the stream with the first streaks of dawn.

I fished for a while and got nothing. It was way too cold for trout fishing (or anything else), but as I've said, Opening Day is a ritual.

It was so cold that there was a skimming of ice on the stagnant water at the bottom of the big pools. It was so cold that ice built up on the line, and inside the guides of the rod. You couldn't fish decently with gloves on, and your fingers got numb if you fished without gloves. You got to shaking because you needed at least two more sweaters than you already had on.

But I had the day to spend, and it was Opening Day, and I tried. I knocked the ice off the guides, and stripped it off the line. I fished grimly.

I came to a deep pool where I had always had good luck. It eddied against a sloping rock. I dropped the worm into the eddy — I was using worms since no fly in his right mind would hatch out under such conditions, and no fish in his right mind would venture up after him if he did — and steered it through the eddy carefully.

I reached out to bring it around just right, and suddenly I felt my feet going out from under me. The moss and the rock had been wet, and the wet had frozen into some of the slipperiest ice it has ever been my bad fortune to encounter.

I sat down hastily and grabbed at everything in the neighborhood. Nothing I could get my hands on had any permanency. I began to slide, slowly at first, the way a giant tree starts its fall under the woodman's ax. Then faster and faster.

Clawing and breaking fingernails on everything near me, I slid majestically into the pool.

I have heard it said that under these conditions your boots, full of water, will weight you down and pull you under and drown you. That drowning bit didn't appeal to me at all. I set myself for the shock of going under and to the bottom. I prepared myself to walk on the bottom if it was necessary, until I could get the short distance to where my head would poke out.

The shock never came. I never got really under. The straps on my boots were pulled tight around my legs, and a lot of air was trapped inside my heavy pants and my jacket and all the clothes I had on.

I went under only about halfway between my waist and my armpits. For one split second I didn't even feel the water until it got through all that clothing. When it did, *that* was a shock, believe me.

I was buoyed up there by all that air like a fat old lady with an innertube around her. I couldn't even start swimming the way you normally would. I had to reach down to paddle. As more and more water got inside and dispelled the air, I sank lower and lower. But the shore was only a few yards distant. Majestically, sticking up there like a cork, I floated myself over to it and waded out.

Obviously this was a sticky situation. I had no car, it was miles to a telephone. Besides, I wanted to fish.

I repaired to the most sheltered place I could find. I took off my boots first and that wasn't easy. Did you ever try to take off a pair of boots half-full of water? The water forms some sort of vacuum and the resulting suction makes the task fit right along with getting your leg out of a quicksand.

I then took off the socks, the jackets, the sweaters, and the longhandled underwear. After that I stood there in that icy morning air, just as I had been when the doctor held me upside down and slapped my bottom, only larger and right side up.

I emptied out the boots. Then I started wringing everything else out. I wrung every last drop out that I could for two reasons; I wanted it out of there, and wringing it hard kept my blood circulating.

I got myself as dry as I could, and I put every-

thing back on. It was unbelievably cold and clammy at first, but my body warmed things up shortly. And at least the clothes acted as wet insulation.

I went back to fishing, testing all rocks for ice before I trusted myself to them. I still had miserable luck. I might very well be catching cold, but it was a cinch I wasn't catching anything else.

Then I met a friend of mine named Ed. He had had the same luck I had had, but he was dry.

"What we need to do is fish a lake," he told me. "In a lake the water temperature wouldn't have dropped as low with this sudden freeze, after the good weather we've been having. What do you say we try Lake Pleiad?"

I didn't mention that I felt I was an authority on the water temperature of that particular brook. I said, "I got no car."

"Come with me."

We drove up the mountain on Route 125. As we neared the top there began to be snow beside the road. Right below Lake Pleiad is nowadays the Middlebury Snow Bowl ski area, and it will have maybe fifty inches of snow up there when there won't be any down in Middlebury.

We had taken for granted that with the warm spring we'd had, all snow up there would be gone. We'd been pretty naïve.

"Anyhow, we can hike through the snow for the half a mile in there. It will be worth the hike to get some fish."

We found that the cold of the night before had made a crust atop some four feet of snow on the Trail. You'd take three steps on the crust, and when you took the fourth step your leg would go through and drop practically the length of it. If you weren't on the alert, this would snap your head forward like the knot on the end of a whip.

You'd retrieve your leg, go a couple more steps. And just when you were lulled into a false sense of security, the other leg would drop in and your head would snap again, jarring your teeth and maybe making you bite your tongue.

We traveled a long, long half-mile in this manner, buoyed up only by the thought of the fine fishing that awaited us.

As we traveled we developed a cunning in that matter of neck-snapping. If you held your neck constantly rigid enough, it lessened the snap. But it gave you a headache right then. And we later found that it made your neck sore for about four days afterward.

There was, too, one other little matter I had to contend with but that Ed didn't. When you have wrung out your clothing and put it back on, you can never get all the water out. It's impossible. So a drop here and a drop there, from your socks, your pants, your shirts and sweaters, and that heavy underwear, finds its way down into the bottom of your boots by force of gravity.

Ordinarily this isn't bad. Your body heat warms it up, and it isn't too uncomfortable. But when, every few steps, your boot goes into snow all over, snow packs around it, immediately the water inside starts to cool down like champagne in an ice bucket. When your legs aren't deep in snow, snow is clinging to the outside of your boot, and the sole of the boot is on crust.

By the time we were halfway in there, I was walking in a quart or more of ice water. To a person reading in a nice warm room with his feet dry, this may not seem like much of a disaster. Let me assure you there is nothing quite like it in the world for exquisite torture. The Inquisition would most certainly have used it if they'd thought of it or if they'd been able to pick up a pair of hip boots and four feet of snow.

But I buoyed myself, as I say, with anticipation.

And then we made the last turn in the trail, and Lake Pleiad lay there before us — a solid sheet of ice. Not just anchor ice. This was the winter's solid stuff. It never had melted up high that way, as we had assumed it had; the way all the lakes down in the valley had melted long since.

We never wet a line. You couldn't have, short of owning an ice chisel. And then there was the trek out with the boot water getting nearer and nearer thirty-two degrees. I felt like yelling out loud under the torture.

I sat on the car seat with my legs stuck out while Ed worried my boots off for me. I wrung out the socks again and the bottoms of my trousers, and put everything back. I felt better after that. We drove back down into the valley.

It was still only about nine-thirty in spite of all that had happened. We began to fish the huge pool at Big Bend.

No luck. The long rock at the head of the pool was comfortable though, and we were loath to leave the place. Our stomachs had for some time back been assuring us with more and more authority that our watches were wrong and that noon had come, so we broke out a sandwich apiece. While I was wringing some of the water out of my sandwiches and the rest of my lunch, Ed let the current carry his worm deep into the pool. And when it stopped and would go no further, he laid the rod down beside him on the rock and we attacked the sandwiches. Ed ate his and I drank mine.

When we were ready to start on, Ed began to reel in. There was a pleasant tugging at the end of his line, and he landed an eleven-inch brookie.

He threw back, and I threw in my line. Nothing happened. We just sat there. After a long time I felt a tug, and I landed a nice brookie. Ed landed one shortly thereafter.

So we settled ourselves on the rock and just allowed our baits to lie on the bottom where the current deposited them. They'd stay there quite a few minutes, then there'd be a bite.

Ed said, "Looks like all the fish in this pool are in one bunch, and we're letting our bait lie there among 'em until looking at it makes even a half-frozen trout hungry."

I'd never fished brookies that way before. But we hadn't found any fish biting anywhere else, so we just sat there. And the fish kept on coming in — not fast, but steadily. The black clouds in the sky increased; we fished on.

You'd be surprised how rapidly fish mount in your creel under such circumstances. The limit at that time was twenty. We passed ten each and it began to snow. Still we sat there.

When we reached twenty apiece it was snowing hard.

I now had my limit, and it was still morning. Marg wasn't due till after five o'clock that after-

noon. Somehow I couldn't cozy up to the idea of sitting around there nearly six hours in a blinding snowstorm, my clothes wet below the armpits.

So I cadged a ride into Middlebury with Ed. And from Middlebury I started to walk toward Addison, where the car would be. It's nine miles from Middlebury to Addison.

I walked. I walked and walked. The boots, and some more seeped-down water in them, got heavier and heavier. Both heels began to chafe in the wet socks and the spots got to feeling as if somebody were holding a match against them. When you're walking a brook to fish, you don't even think about it. When you're walking just to get somewhere, you think about nothing else.

The twenty brook trout in the creel, which had at first seemed only pleasantly heavy, went rapidly through various stages until I'd have sworn each fish was eight times its size and made of lead.

I walked six miserable miles, and only the first one held itself down to a mere 5,280 feet. I got a ride the last three miles, and only the fact that the driver who stopped and picked me up was sitting in his car kept me from dropping to my knees and kissing his feet.

But the strange part is that after I got dry, and the blisters healed, I found that I'd had a wonderful time. I wouldn't have missed it for the world. In the years to come it took its place as one of the nicest days I ever spent. This doesn't seem either reasonable or sensible. But that's how it was.

*Dorset Mt.,
by Arthur Griffin*

A Manchester Brook, by John Harris

A Yellow Towhee Sings in a Budded Tree and a Grosbeak and a Scarlet Tanager perch in new Leaves, by Ernest Gay

Moss Glen Falls, Granville Gulf, by Dick Smith

Cilley Bridge, Tunbridge, by Lud Munchmeyer

A Field of Golden Dandelions in Wilmington and a
Country Road South of Arlington, by H. Stanley Johnson

summer

Atop Mt. Mansfield,
by Clyde Smith

Peacham Village,
by Winston Pote

Floating Bridge,
Brookfield, by Arthur Griffin

Gulls in Flight, Lake Champlain, by Bullaty-Lomeo

Morning Mist, Waterbury, by John H. Vondell

Heron in a Bog near Bradford, by Charles C. Johnson

Otter Creek Valley from the Landgrove to Mt. Tabor Road and a view from the top of Bromley to Stratton Mt., by Ernest Gay

Camel's Hump from the Molly Stark Balcony, Long Trail, by John H. Vondell

Tree Swallow, by Ernest Gay

Long Shadows on Hazen's Notch near Lowell, and Dusk at Joe's Pond, West Danville, by Bullaty-Lomeo

Buswell's Pond, Plymouth,
by Richard Frutchey

They Settled the Hills

RALPH N. HILL

About eleven o'clock in the morning we set out [from Crown Point] with a fair wind. On both sides of the lake are high chains of mountains. On the eastern shore is a low piece of ground covered with a forest, extending between nine to twelve English miles, after which the mountains begin, and the country beyond them belongs to New England. This chain consists of high mountains, which are to be considered as the boundaries between the French and English possessions in these parts of North America.

The lake at first is but a French mile broad but keeps increasing in size afterwards. The country is inhabited within a French mile of the fort, but after that it is covered with a thick forest. At a distance of about ten French miles from Fort St. Frédéric, the lake is four such miles broad and we perceived some islands in it. This day the sky was cloudy and the clouds, which were very low, seemed to surround several high mountains near the lake with a fog. From many mountains the fog rose, as the smoke of a charcoal kiln. Now and then we saw a little river which emptied into the lake.

We often saw Indians in bark boats close to the shore, which was, however, not inhabited, for the Indians came here only to catch sturgeons wherewith this lake abounds and which we often saw leaping up into the air. These Indians lead a very singular life. At one time of the year they live on the small store of corn, beans, and melons which they have planted; during another period, or about this time, their food is fish, without bread or any other meat; and another season they eat nothing but game such as stags, roes, beavers, etc., which they shoot in the woods and rivers. They, however, enjoy long life, perfect health, and are more able to undergo hardships than other people. They sing and dance, are joyful and always content, and would not for a great deal exchange their manner of life for that which is preferred in Europe.

— *Peter Kalm, 1749*

In the course of this summer I took a singular stroll. I took six days of provisions in my pack, a small pocket pistol, little horn of powder, and a hatchet of a small size for the benefit of making fire, and set out to view the country a little to the North of Hubbardton. One evening I had made a fire and as there appeared a prospect of rain I had cut some crotches and stretched my blanket to keep off the rain, and cut some hemlock boughs for a bed, and laid down for repose, when I was soon disturbed by hearing thunder at a distance, preceded by the roaring of a tremendous wind. The falling of trees was incessant and I found the hurricane was coming directly to me. I had little time for consideration. I recollected seeing a large pine that was turned up by the roots, and at about eight feet lay firm on the ground, a safe retreat if all the trees in the woods were turned up by the roots. I had possession of my new habitation when the wind, rain, thunder and lightning reached the place. A great many trees and branches of trees were brought to the ground and some fell on every side of my fire. One tree fell across the log under which I lay a little distance from me. The storm was soon over. I repaired my fire and slept very comfortably the remainder of the night.

Two days after the hurricane I ascended a high

precipice or top of a mountain east of a long pond, the source of Hubbardton River in said town, where I found a great prospect to view the adjoining country. The day being clear and air pure contributed much to my prospect of learning from the top of a tall spruce tree, which stood within thirty feet of a ledge I judged to be at least 300 feet perpendicular. I had a small compass in my pocket and hatchet in my hand and climbed to the top of the tree. With the hatchet I cut off the top and trimmed it to answer as a compass staff, and placed my compass on it, turning and viewing lands at a great distance. While thus amusing myself, the day being some windy, a sudden gust of wind caused the top of the tree to wave over the ledge. At this unlucky moment I chanced to cast my eyes down the tree, waved by the wind over. It had the appearance that I was going to the bottom. This gave me sensations not easily expressed. Let it suffice to say it caused a general chill to the motion of the blood — a strong feeling in my head and heart, with weakness in my limbs, at which prudence dictated to me to put the compass instantly into my pocket, and go down the tree. I went about two thirds down, stopped, and, on a few minutes reflection, came to my usual feelings. I then considered that the wind was not so high as at many other times, that I must be unlucky indeed if the tree fell in the time necessary for me to take minutes of the lands in the adjacent country. I resumed my courage and went and set my compass on the top of said tree, and with my pen made regular minutes of my discoveries without looking down till my business was finished. From such a view I could gain as much general knowledge of the country as by a week's traveling through the low lands.

The fifth day of my stroll I was on the top of another high ledge. After climbing a tree and viewing the country I came down and discovered a large stone I could easily roll off, which for amusement I did, and several others. A little down the side of the first mentioned steep part of the rock lay a rock twice as big as a hogshead, and apparently easily turned off. I viewed it for some time and then ventured down, taking off my shoes. I was very cautious observing small bushes that grew out of the cracks of the rocks, and one just by the stone I wished to roll. I went back and cut two pries, there being a place I could put them under, and put my feet on the ends, so that I made use of both strength and heft to turn the rock off. By this means I turned it. A craggy piece of the rock that projected towards me, and which I took hold of when the rock moved, came against me as I was stooping over it lifting, and came near throwing me over the rock. I, by exertion, extracted myself, caught by the large bush aforesaid, and staid quiet where I was. But the danger I had escaped greatly eclipsed my pleasure in seeing the rock roll. But it went with tremendous force; and striking other rocks in its descent, raised a strong sulphurous smell, and when it came to the standing timber it cut its way like a bush scythe, carrying with it the butts of trees, their tops falling up the hill. This would have been a pleasant sight to me on a safe ground. I moved carefully to the top of the hill, and have been extremely careful in rolling rocks from such heights ever since.

— Ira Allen, 1772

Vermont has been settled entirely from the other States of New-England. In the formation of Colonies those who are first inclined to emigrate are usually such as have met with difficulties at home. These are commonly joined by persons who, having large families and small farms, are induced for the sake of settling their children comfortably to seek for new and cheaper lands. To both are always added the discontented, the enterprizing, the ambitious, and the covetous.

A considerable part of all who begin the cultivation of the wilderness may be denominated foresters or Pioneers. The business of these persons is no other than to cut down trees, build log-houses, lay open forested grounds to cultivation, and prepare the way for those who come after them. These men cannot live in regular society. They are too idle, too talkative, too passionate, too prodigal, and too shiftless to acquire property or character. They are impatient of the restraints of law, religion, and morality; grumble about the taxes by which Rulers, Ministers, and Schoolmasters are supported; and complain incessantly, as well as bitterly, of the extortions of mechanics, farmers, merchants, and physicians; to whom they are always indebted. After displaying their own talents and worth, after censuring the weakness and wickedness of their superiors, they become at length discouraged, and under the pressure of poverty, the fear of a gaol, and the consciousness of public contempt, leave their native places and betake themselves to the wilderness.

— *Timothy Dwight, 1810*

In great contrast to this extensive open forest land [of the hills] was the tangled wilds that overspread the valleys of the streams. There everything looked dark and peculiarly forbidding. There the evergreens of black timber such as hemlock, spruce and fir prevailed, and were thickly intermingled with birch, ash and elm; while a heavy and almost impervious growth of all sorts of underbrush gave the whole the appearance of a black, gloomy and impassable mass of woods. And besides this these tangled forests were found, when land-lookers or others succeeded in penetrating them, to be often so wet and swampy as to deter most emigrants from any attempt to clear them up for settlement. What wonder then that they so generally preferred to make drier pitches on the higher grounds. As the event proved, however, in clearing up the whole country, the settlers greatly underrated the value and feasibility of the low lands. For when the sun was once let in, and these dark masses of forest and the roots and stumps were rotted, the lowlands made beautiful, easy-wrought and productive meadows.

It now seems a singular fact that the first settlers of this State should have so generally pitched on the highest plains and plateaus, miles from any water power, for villages which they evidently supposed must become centres of population and seats of public business. A few of these upland villages, like Randolph Centre, Peacham and Danville, have made shift to retain there the locations of meeting-houses and academies, but that seems to have been about all. Their populations have been stationary or decreasing, while their business has nearly all gone down to the banks of the nearest rivers where thriving villages have sprung up, all seeming to begin alike and grow by the same natural process. In the first place a grist-mill and saw-mill were found to be matters of indispensable necessity. These of themselves became unavoidably places of resort and most favorable for seeing people from all other parts of the town. Hence soon followed the shoemaker, blacksmith, and soon the tavern-keeper and the merchant. And the nucleus of a village being thus formed, the place at once began to draw away the population of the hill village and grow to an important place of business. Such has proved so often the case that it may now be considered a settled matter that no village can long sustain itself or become a place of much importance located far aloof from good water-power.

— *Daniel P. Thompson, circa 1868*

Early Morning near North Troy, by Grant Heilman

The McLam Farm, East Topsham, by Hanson Carroll

That's How It Was

MURRAY HOYT

A sweet young thing in her early teens said to me this summer, "Mr. Hoyt, *you* must remember way, *way* back when there was just nothing interesting going on in the world; no outer space program, no television, no radio even, no cars, no fast boats or water skiing, no tractors, no movies, no running-water, no plumbing, just *nothing*."

"Would you believe," I asked her, "that George Washington and I used to commiserate with each other about that very situation?"

And she said, "Oh, *you*! But seriously, whatever did people *do*? How did they get around? Especially way up here in Vermont away from everywhere? And with nobody earning much money?"

I went home and thought about this a lot. Several generations have come along whose members have no first-hand knowledge of what life with low earnings and without modern inventions was like. They feel sorry for us, probably rightly, for having been born too soon.

So this, Virginia, is my attempt to show you how awful it really was.

Beginning when I was two years old, I spent my summers with my family on Lake Champlain in our cottage at Potash Bay. Today there are two dozen or more cottages along the shores of Potash Bay, but at that time ours was the only one. It was set on corner rocks and was made of novelty siding on studding. There was no road to it; we had to reach it through a gate and along the edge of a hayfield. The gate had to be kept closed for fear cows might get into the meadow and trample the hay. The trip through the hayfield was about a quarter of a mile.

The cottage had a huge screened porch on which my parents and I did most of our living and where we slept at night. There was a large living room with fireplace, a tiny kitchen, and four bedrooms upstairs. The plumbing wasn't. Its place was taken by a small building known by the somewhat less-than-frank title of "woodshed". Lake water was forced up into a storage tank on the second floor by a one-manpower pump, and from there reached a single faucet in the kitchen below by gravity. Any hot water was heated on the kitchen oil stove in a teakettle.

Similar cottages along Potash Bay today are sold at a figure between five thousand and ten thousand dollars. In 1907 my parents had spent the then magnificent sum of $100 to build these buildings.

I thought, very simply, that it was paradise. My father had been born and spent his boyhood near that cottage, but by that time he was the head of the English Department at Clark University. Therefore we lived in Worcester, Massachusetts during the school year.

For weeks before our leaving Worcester for the summer I planned and dreamed of the camp and the lake, and I'd pack fishing tackle and other things that mattered, days in advance of our scheduled departure.

We got up very early on the chosen morning, and rode on a trolley to Union Depot where we boarded the train for Winchendon. At Winchendon we changed to the Boston section of the rather optimistically titled "Green Mountain Flyer".

My father always found two green plush-cushioned seats together and turned over the

Barnet,
by Winston Pote

back of one so that we could sit together. The hours dragged, but were helped in their passing by trips to the water cooler in the end of the coach.

The large box-luncheon which my mother had put up, we ate at noon. There was a diner, but the prices charged "were outrageous, actually sometimes as much as *two whole dollars* for just a dinner" and the box lunch was our answer. We finally reached Vergennes, Vermont in mid-afternoon.

Here we were met by a farmer with a pair of horses and a double wagon. We bought a long list of groceries at Dalrymple's Store, sometimes as much as five dollars' worth, but of course some of those staples would last all summer. These groceries we loaded into the wagon and we started our ten mile ride to the lake. It was slow going; the horses trotted some on the level, but walked far too much to suit me. We moved at about four miles an hour. When we reached the watering trough on Creamery Hill in Addison, the driver got out and loosened the check rein and the horses drank.

These were Morgans, and would be hitched to a hay rack to pull huge loads of hay the next day. But before that day's work started, my father and I would go up to the farmer's barn where our boat had been kept during the winter, help load it onto the hay rack and drive it to the lake. There the horses would back the wagon a bumpy, scary distance out into the water, and we would slide the boat off until it floated, and row it to our beach.

Those first nights were always so still it was hard to sleep out there on the screened porch. No sound of trolleys, no noises of those new contraptions called automobiles. The splash of a fish feeding late, perhaps. Sometimes there'd be the imbecile laugh of a loon, or the squawk of a heron, or, if the wind was right, the sound of sheep or cows in a distant pasture.

We always took a quick dip in the lake before we dressed in the morning. We did this raw. Even when we had guests, that was the procedure. And my parents had a lot of guests just as anyone living next to a lake always does; sometimes all four rooms upstairs were full. There was a lot of gaiety and laughter and give-and-take because these people didn't seem to realize there was nothing to do. The bathing area couldn't be seen down over the cliff from the cottage and the women were supposed to go down in bathrobes, and when they had all returned the men all went down in bathrobes. We laid these aside and we swam in the all-together. And nobody was supposed to peek, and to the best of my knowledge nobody ever did. There were no boats or cottages around and it kept our bathing suits dry for the before-dinner swim.

We fished every morning except Sundays. My father bought milk at a farm a mile away by water — five cents a quart — and we'd troll over and back using bamboo-pole outriggers. My father always said it gave him a perfect excuse to fish regularly.

We did very well with the fishing. We ate fish nearly every day for two reasons; it was good, and meat was hard for us to buy or to keep fresh. We had to walk about five miles to the nearest grocery store by land, but by water we could row about four miles to stores in Port Henry, New

York. So we didn't do much tripping to the store for meat. In addition to the northern pike that we caught trolling, we still-fished for perch, sheepshead, bass and other varieties, in the late afternoons.

There was one meat cart which came around once each week. If you phoned them the day before, they'd bring along any groceries you wanted them to bring. But since we had to walk up and meet the cart at the road, and also because telephoning was such an emotional experience, we used this service sparingly.

Telephoning; now there was something. You walked up to the nearest farmhouse that had a phone and you picked up the receiver from a hook on the side of the wooden-box on the wall. The mouthpiece stuck out at you on a metal arm. You heard all sorts of ghost voices; it was nearly impossible to tell whether one set of voices was loud enough to mean your line was being used.

If you thought it wasn't, you held down the receiver and cranked the crank on the side of the box the requisite number of longs and shorts to get the party you were after. Then there was a lot of shouting. The voice you heard wasn't much louder than the other ghost voices, and there was much, "What? What? Louder; I can't hear you." Usually you were able to get your message across; sometimes you weren't and the farmer's wife graciously agreed to call later and relay the message when the telephone was less noisy. Or when less people were listening-in and cutting down the volume. "Listening-in" every time the phone rang was a way of life in the country.

About once a week there'd be a "sociable" at the Community House. Or there'd be a church-sponsored "entertainment" to raise money for the "Ladies Aid". My father gave readings, my mother was a trained musician, so the church would be anxious enough for us to perform so that they'd have someone stop for us with a horse and carriage. The ice cream was yellow and smooth from the heavy rich cream used, and it had been made in an ice cream freezer the handle of which had been turned by hand, while salt and last winter's lake ice from an icehouse were packed in around the whirling container with its "dasher" turning inside. It was a kid's job to lick off the dasher when it was removed from the finished product, a delightful chore.

Most evenings we read by kerosene lamps and went to bed early, sleepy from the sun and the swimming and the exercise. We got up early each morning. On Sundays and on rainy days there were a lot of rowboats trolling. The farmers had no cars and town was a long way away. So they fished on rainy days. They never fish now.

On good days, in haying season, some farmer friend would get caught with a lot of hay down and come and ask my father if he'd help by pitching hay the next day. My father would, and I would be allowed to ride on the load of hay and drive the horses from one haycock to the next. And to "tread" the wonderful smelling hay in the mow as it was being "pitched off". There would be a huge meal of fricasseed chicken at noon, and between loads the farmer and my father and I would drink an iced thirst-quencher made of water with ginger in it. This was considered more effective on a hot day than plain water.

Except for boats that rowed past on Sundays and rainy days, we'd see no one, week in and week out, except those who came to see us. The side-wheel steamer *Vermont* would go by about eleven o'clock each day on its trip from Plattsburgh to Ticonderoga and return, and we knew exactly how many minutes it would be before her wake would have crossed a couple of miles of water and would crash against our shore. Once in a while the steamer *Ticonderoga* would come down on a moonlight excursion, dock at Loomis' dock two miles above us and unload apple barrels. We'd see her lights round Barber's Point near Westport, and we'd row up to Loomis' dock and sit in the dark in our skiff and watch the excitement and the running stevedores with their small-wheeled dollies. There was often an orchestra playing for dancing on the after deck. It was very gay.

Once each summer there'd be an excursion from Port Henry and we'd row over and go on it. When the *Ti* returned to port she'd "blow" the contents of her firebox. Huge jets of live coals would shoot out from her side and hiss into the water. Afterward we'd row home in the night, and the D&H train sliding along its track close to the water would look like a lighted snake. It was a very amazing feeling to a small boy to watch it and wonder who was on it and where they were going.

We'd gather wild strawberries for shortcake, later wild raspberries and blackberries. We'd hunt bees on a pleasant afternoon. Now and then we'd have to walk to where the "cream wagon", which collected cream from the farms for the creamery in Addison, was kept at night. On a certain day each week creamery butter was left in one of the containers for us.

Once we paddled to Vergennes, up Otter Creek, to get an ice cream sundae, a roundabout distance of thirty-six miles for the day. We went on picnics by boat or canoe. On the Fourth of July we always roamed out into the lake after dark far enough so that we could watch the fireworks display at Port Henry and at Westport and Basin Harbor, all at the same time. Coming home from still-fishing, across the bay after dark, sometimes my mother would sing if the night was still. As the summer drew to a close and our remaining days became few, I'd sit up in the bow where nobody could see me plainly, and maybe shed a silent tear or two because I wanted so badly to stay longer in that lovely place. I remember this poignantly.

All too soon would come the last day, and the hay rack to pick up the boat, over where the road dipped down next to the lake. Last of all we put on the blinds. And then the horses and the wagon would come to take us to Vergennes and the train to take us back to Worcester.

The groceries for the whole summer cost less than twenty dollars, and if it hadn't been for all the entertaining, would have been far less even than that.

As I think back on it, there must have been something wrong with me not to need a car or a motorcycle or a speedboat or a radio or a television set or lots of money. But even though it shows me as being a person who didn't know enough to miss the good and interesting things in life, anyway that's how it was.

Mill Pond, East Calais, by John F. Smith

Hiking Atop Mt. Mansfield, by John H. Vondell

Lazy Summer Day in Pawlet, by Clyde Smith

South Wardsboro Reflections, by John Harris

Indian Paint Brush, West Dover,
by Lawrence McDonald

Middlebury Congregational Church,
by John F. Smith

Cycling through Lower Waterford and a
Sailing Race on Lake Champlain, near Shelburne, by Hanson Carroll

Connecticut River at Fairlee, by Ruth Archer

Escape to Vermont

WALTER R. HARD, JR.

Well before the Civil War Summer visitors had begun arriving in the remote Green Mountains by train, to partake of the curative waters at pioneering mineral spring resorts. By the turn of the century, Vermont hill farm homes, which took in summer boarder refugees from the baking cities, were finding it provided a fairly healthy boost to farm income.

But the great floods of city visitors, now with new cars, new cash and the leisure to employ both, grew apace beyond most natives' wildest hopes (or fears) when World War II ended. Year by year more and more of them became part-time residents or determined transplants.

These new Vermonters brought with them new concepts of living, and new economic and political tenets which were alien to the older residents. Local attitudes, however, had moderated considerably in the fifteen years since Bernard DeVoto observed that Vermont "has no intention of altering its provincial culture and provincial point of view," a tenacity which he admired.

The balance between old and new was teetering by mid-century under the sheer number of recent arrivals. "Newcomers found the native Vermonters a different breed," wrote Earle W. Newton. "— one often hard to understand. Some returned disillusioned to the bars and beauty shops of 'civilization' after a brief flirtation with 'country life'. But others made a successful readjustment to a different way of life, and soon found its more leisurely pace and even its stubborn conservatism not unattractive.

"Because the influx contained a large proportion of artists and writers, the nation was soon treated to an intensive interpretation of the Vermont way of life on canvas and paper. The spate of books about an author's new home in the country, or his frustrations but eventual contentment in the restoration of an old house, finally brought the expected sour response, when someone wrote a volume entitled *Escape from Vermont*.

"The unique qualities and values of the Green Mountain state found ardent exponents in the new immigrants, who interpreted Vermont to the nation through their works, and vastly enriched its cultural heritage thereby. There are no more violent defenders of 'unspoiled Vermont' than the late denizens of various Baghdads-on-the-subway."

A somewhat more trenchant view of Vermont's new dichotomy came from expatriate Vermonter Burges Johnson: "Dyed in the wool Vermonters are easily recognizable after a brief scrutiny and the exchange of only a few words. This does not apply to summer residents or imported hermits who have come to write books. There is a Vermont saying that if a cat has kittens in the oven we do not necessarily call them biscuits."

Writer Miriam Chapin, however, came recklessly to grips in 1957 with what was happening to the sloganed "Vermont way of life." As a sixth-generation Vermonter, she declared that Vermont has been conquered by the cities, and is a fief of Boston and New York. "It is about time," she wrote, "Vermonters came out from their maple sugar bush, out from under the covered bridge, took off their patchwork quilts, and looked themselves in the eye. The process of taking over the Green Mountains as an annex of Bronxville and Brookline has been going on for considerably more than fifty years, but since 1945 it has been precipitous."

Citing the decline of farming, the re-growth of the forests and the coming of industry, Mrs. Chapin noted that "Vermont has only two colonies of the very rich, Manchester and Woodstock — and a few isolated big estates. Most of the farms have gone to professional people and the middle class. None of them has any real contact with the local people. None of them knows what it is like to live all winter in a house heated by wood stoves, all are distrusted in greater or less degree by their native neighbors, who make what they can out of them.

"Not only are the summer owners increasing each year, but the big corporations are happily moving in. The young executives delight in fixing up old houses for their homes. But they have no real stake in the community."

Reporting later on conditions at Huntington, juxtaposed to now-burgeoning Burlington, Don Wakefield wrote in *The Nation:* "The town . . . like so many others, will be eventually over-run by the spreading Megalopolis. Now it simply waits for the neon future, while its farms turn into real estate and its residents turn into commuters."

Mrs. Chapin's views, singularly unappreciated at home, were followed a year later by the more moderate words of former-Vermonter, Robert L. Duffus, a *New York Times* editor who prefaced a recollection of his Vermont boyhood with the disclaimer: "I do not try to pass judgment on where the balance lies, but I do not wish to be listed among those ancient parties who nostalgically worship an ancient past. Life was better there (*Williamstown in the '90s*) in some respects than it is in most parts of the world today. It was worse in other respects."

Murmuring Pines and Martinis

Groton State Forest: On the basis of a brief sojourn in the heart of this well-tracked wilderness, it may be stated that the definitive means of getting close to nature these days, without coming to grips with it, is to go camping. Nobody chews pemmican or gnaws on edible roots and only a handful of eccentrics and antiquarians invite their souls on a bed of boughs beneath the murmuring pines and hemlocks, bearded with moss, and so on. By and large the great outdoors has been carefully curried, paved, padded, motorized, trailerized, electrified, sprayed, shower-bathed, washing-machined, flush-toileted and here and there cocktail-lounged, the sorry scheme of Things entire shattered to bits by bulldozers and then remolded nearer to the Heart's desire.

In fact, if figures are any indication, it is so much nearer the Heart's desire that more people will buddy up to more of the New Nature this summer than at any time in the history of the republic.

But these are only numbers, dry bones, adumbrations or, as Longfellow put it in another connection, "Still stands the forest primeval; but under the shade of its branches/ Dwell another race, with other customs and language." Give or take a few amenities, Groton State Forest, a demesne of 16,000 acres, is pretty much typical of all state and national parks. Matters have come to such a pretty pass indeed at Groton State that not only may camp sites be reserved in advance, but they had better be.

The last decade has recorded, as well, astonishing rises in the sales and varieties of camping equipment, all of it cunningly designed to keep the elements at arm's length, the effect being something like watching a Burton Holmes travelogue at a drive-in theater during a thunderstorm.

Spring water has been run into Groton and all the outdoor man has to do to get it is drive possibly a hundred feet to a faucet atop a pipe rising out of the ground. Extremely attractive wash houses in brown, with blue doors, contain showers, flush toilets, dressing tables for the ladies, tubs for laundry, mirrors, electric lights and outlets for electric shavers.

Vermont has stopped short of hot water, but it has been inordinately generous with wood. Wood is not only free once the camper gets into the forest, but it is cut, sorted into convenient sizes, depending upon the kind of fire one intends to build, and piled in clearings. Very likely the most stunning aspect of these woodlots is that half the logs come from somewhere else. The forest people buy waste pieces from a bobbin mill in Groton.

Groton's wood is so highly thought of that every now and then the campers try to sneak out with a station-wagonful. They are stopped at the little white huts called "contact stations" and told to put it back.

The principal occupation of today's camper is to do nothing assiduously, as a visitor discovered after tramping conscientiously through Groton State in search of activity. A little fishing is done, a little walking, some visiting back and forth. Every now and then somebody gets up a bridge game that leaves the participants exhausted by cocktail time.

Almost nobody gets up in the morning before 9 or 10 o'clock. About the only exception to this was the camper whose lean-to was located near a woodpile. He was awakened the other day shortly before 7:30 a.m. by the clunk of a dull ax belaboring a piece of wood. Upon extracting himself from his sleeping bag, he stumbled into the sunlight to find an 8-year-old boy working over a log. The boy said he had got up early and tried to rouse his father. He had been told to go get the ax and chop. It would be good for his muscles.

"As you get older," said one experienced camper, "you get to tolerate the comforts." Others detected in themselves a struggling up to the surface of some past memories of the days when life was real and earnest and things had to be done with the hands. To them modern camp-ing was a return to the soil — in the fashion, of course, of Marie Antoinette pushing sheep around with a golden crook in the Petit Trianon.

Still others saw the urge as a splendid way to keep the family together on vacation, instead of sending the children off to organized camps and going to a hotel themselves. A number of women gave in, they said, on the theory that since their husbands were bent and determined, it was better to join them since they couldn't be beaten. The women, however, have exacted a most subtle sort of payment in return — they are unquestionably responsible for all the improvements that have been made in the real thing. Lastly, camping is demonstrably cheaper.

That evening, hard by a Jaguar and two Cadillacs from out of state, Mrs. Harry Seivwright of Montpelier recalled that as a child she had submitted to camping the hard way. "I wouldn't do it now," she said. "We do this because Harry gets restless in a cottage or hotel. This seems to be the only way he's willing to do nothing and relax. Here you enjoy doing nothing more. Besides there isn't anything to do and you don't feel guilty at not having anything to do. The only embarrassing thing is trying to tell people what you did when you get home." The Seivwrights were giving dinner for a guest — nothing elaborate. Seivwright broke out a bottle of Canadian whiskey, one of Scotch and one of gin. He produced vermouth for martinis from an old coffee pot.

Mrs. Seivwright opened a can of smoked oysters and one of sardines. She laid out a box of sesame crackers and one of ordinary biscuits. A pound of store cheese — unpretentious, but somehow compelling — was thrown in by a neighboring couple who drifted over for drinks on invitation.

There was not a single mosquito around; the few deer flies there seemed disinclined to make trouble. A man named Andrew Lyons from Springfield, Mass., ambled up with a plastic bag of ice cubes. The Seivwrights had plenty of ice cubes in a plastic bucket, but they thanked him nonetheless. In the course of the cocktail-party chit-chat that ensued, Lyons remarked that he had to drive half a mile from his tent to a store in the forest to get the cubes. "You've got to take the bitter with the sweet," he conceded.

Like everyone else, Lyons had a portable icebox, but he was reluctant to make work for himself by chipping pieces off the block it accommodates. At the same time he felt that those electric refrigerators that can be plugged into an automobile battery, or as in the case of some forests other than Groton, to electrical outlets tacked to the trees, were a little effete.

"I had to go into town the other day," Lyons said, "to drop off a couple of loads at the laundromat and pick up some things at the supermarket. Pure hell. It was so hot, I pretty near died; I had to stand in line at the checkout counter. And that reminds me — I'm down to half a bottle of Tom Collins mix."

Mrs. Seivwright tossed a salad delicately, her husband attended to the steaks and Lyons provided a visitor with one poignant clue of what draws people to this simulacrum of pioneering.

"I travel a lot," he said. "I'm in hotels a good deal, go to a lot of nice places, but after a while, the food tastes like sawdust, no matter how good it is. I remember one convention we had in Miami Beach. A real rat race. A million people on the beach. You couldn't even see the ocean, let alone relax. I get up here and have spaghetti and hot dogs and it tastes real good."

— *Gilbert Millstein*

autumn

Maple Leaves, by Ernest Gay

Hazen Road, Mosquitoville,
in Barnet, by Bullaty-Lomeo

East Topsham, by Hans Wendler

Pleasant Valley Morning, by Dick Smith

Lone Rider, Upper Hollow, Strafford, by Hanson Carroll

Early Autumn, a Gorge in Woodstock, by Carlos Elmer

Quechee Gorge, by Ruth Archer

Golden Elm, Jeffersonville, by Dick Smith

Ottauquechee Reflections, Bridgewater, by Jack Breed

A Farm near Passumpsic, by Jack Breed

Tree Farm, West Woodstock, by David Witham

Sugarhouse in Cambridge, by Robert Hagerman

Factory Brook, Barnet,
by David Witham

Autumn's Bright Harvest

RALPH N. HILL

After dinner we set out for Manchester and, having rode two miles, were obliged to shelter ourselves from a violent rain in a saddler's shop. Here we continued till sun set and then returned to the inn at which we had dined. The building stood on a handsome elevation overlooking an extensive valley toward the East, and gave us a full prospect of the Green Mountain range for a great distance.

The wind blew violently from the North West. The heavens were dark; the clouds were wild, tossed in fantastical forms. Many of them struck the mountains at their middle height and thence sailed up their bosom with a motion which, notwithstanding their rapid progress over our heads, was to our eyes, slow, majestic, and awful. The world was universally wrapt in gloom and the bosom of the mountain was covered with a deep brown, approaching to black. After this melancholy and cavern-like darkness had continued about one hour; and tempest and tumult appeared to reign universally, suddenly most beautiful and brilliant spots of gold of various figures and sizes formed by the light of the sun piercing through the interstices of the clouds, were seen wandering over the surface of the valley beneath; crossing the farms, houses, and forests; slowly ascending the acclivities of the mountains; gradually sliding over the summits; and thus fading, successively, from sight. The contrast between the gloom and the splendour was so strong; the splendour itself was in many instances so vivid (for the spots were not equally bright and on that account were, in a group, more beautiful) that they appeared as if the vallies, farms, forests, and mountains, were succes-sively polished and luminous. I never beheld any prospect more striking, or more complete.

—Timothy Dwight, 1798

The farm we have purchased is in a retired spot upon the brow of a large hill about one mile from the [West] Brattleborough meeting house. We have wheat and rye now in the ground and promising a sufficiency of those grains for our bread and pies. We have two large orchards and two smaller ones coming on, and expect to make some fifty or sixty barrels of cider. We have plenty of good pasturing and hay enough to winter thirty head of cattle. With the farm we purchased farming tools, young cattle, hogs, poultry, and twenty-three sheep who have now increased the flock by eight lambs, and it would amuse you to see Sophia and the children surrounded with sheep, lambs, geese, turkeys and hens, feeding them from their hands.

The house [has] a handsome portico, two handsome front rooms, well finished, papered and painted, and two handsome chambers over them; back is a sitting-room and by the side of it a room for my office, back of the sitting-room a good kitchen, from whence you go into two bed-rooms, one for the boys and the other for the maids, and overhead a meal granary; and over the sitting-room an apartment for our hired man and boy. Back of the kitchen is a long wood-house, about twenty feet of which makes a summer washroom, and here stands the water-trough, constantly supplied with plenty·of ex-cellent water.

In front of the house is a fruit garden, peaches, plums, etc., but the former will not bear until

next year. On one side of the house is a kitchen garden with a good asparagus bed and plenty of currants, red, white and black, and large English gooseberries; on the other side is a flower garden. Next to the house runs a small brook, on the other side of which is a grass plot set out with young fruit trees, chiefly plums. We have on the place a plenty of common cherry trees and four fine blackheart cherry trees near the front windows. We have also pear trees which bear, and quince bushes. On the place we may gather cartloads of chestnuts, no walnuts, but a sufficiency of butternuts. In a word, if one can love a retired farmer's life, here you may have it to perfection.
— *Royall Tyler, 1801*

From Fort Ticonderoga we soon crossed the lake and landed at the station of Shoreham. About three o'clock the steam-boat *Burlington* stopped at the landing-place and in her we embarked for Burlington, higher up Lake Champlain, where we proposed to land. This was one of the most elegant vessels I had yet seen in America; and of steam-vessels the most complete in all her fittings and equipments that I had ever seen in any part of the world, not excepting the *Great Western*, which I visited and examined at New York.

The *Burlington* being built for lake navigation and not having to encounter the heavy gales of the Atlantic, did not, of course, require the strength and solidity of the *Great Western*; and this enabled her constructors to give her a finer mould and to produce elegance of form and rapidity of motion in a higher degree. Her hull is a complete model of grace and beauty; all her equipments are of the first order and her interior accommodation, for comfort and spendour combined, surpass those of any ship or vessel I have ever seen. The captain was worthy of his ship, taking the highest degree of pride in her, and every part of her was as sweet, pure, and clean as a royal yacht.

At eight o'clock we reached Burlington, where we landed and reposed for the night, the steam-boat pursuing her way to the head of Lake Champlain at St. John's, where the greater number of her passengers would disembark for Montreal. Having secured an extra coach with four beautiful horses and a smart driver, we left Burlington after breakfast for Montpelier, the capital of the State of Vermont. Our way was through the most beautiful scenery, amid the green hills which induced the original French settlers of this territory to call it the land of the Green Mountains, a name it well deserves. The continued succession of these beautiful hills, with the intervening valleys and plains by which they were divided from each other, made every mile of our ride delightful. The most romantic parts of [England's] Derbyshire and the richest parts of Devonshire are not so lovely as the hills and valleys of this part of Vermont, in which there is every element of landscape beauty, and every combination of the picturesque.

The hills are clothed with wood to the very summits, a great portion of which are evergreens. The plains are covered with the richest carpets of meadowgrass; and cattle of the finest description were grazing in luxuriant abundance. Sometimes a new feature of beauty would burst in a frowning perpendicular cliff or a projecting mass of naked rock, peering out from amidst the thick foliage by which it was surrounded, and then the perpetually winding river, appearing and disappearing at every turn, would vary the scene.

The gorgeous colouring of an American autumn added a still greater charm to this enchanting picture, and we sometimes found it difficult to persuade ourselves that the deep rich browns, bright yellows, and deep blood-crimsons and scarlets of the trees we saw before us, mingled with the richest greens of every tint and hue, could be really natural or without the aid of art, it looked so like the artificial dying or colouring of some great manufactory, except that the colours were more varied, more brilliant, and more vivid than any art can produce. Altogether it was one of the most beautiful tracts of country through which we had yet passed, and alone quite worth a voyage across the Atlantic to see and enjoy.

After passing through the villages of Richmond and Waterbury, at each of which we changed horses, we reached Montpelier at half-past one, having performed the distance of 40 miles in less than five hours, being the most expeditious rate at which we had yet travelled for any distance by land. Montpelier is the legislative capital of the State of Vermont and is one of the prettiest towns of its size that can be imagined. The most elegant building is the State-House, in which the legislature of Vermont hold their sittings. This is constructed in the best taste as a work of architecture, and its classic portico and graceful dome are in the best proportions; the material is a fine grey granite of even texture and uniform colour, and the workmanship of the most perfect kind.

After dining agreeably at an excellent hotel we took a fresh extra-coach for Danville, where we intended to sleep. In the course of our first stage we came to one of the many wooden bridges with which the country abounds, now in the act of being repaired, and apparently impassable, as the flooring or platform of the bridge, consisting of loose planks, had all been removed. But the driver, with great good humour and alacrity, set to work himself to place the planks across again in their proper places, and in the course of half an hour the bridge was sufficiently restored for us to pass in safety. This driver, like all we had seen in America, was remarkably kind to his horses, and though he drove faster and steadier than any who had yet driven us, he never used his whip to touch the horses, but merely smacked it in the air and talked to the animals as though he believed they understood every word he said. I may add that while the American drivers appear to be uniformly kind, the horses themselves are more docile and tractable than with us, and up to the present time, at least, we have met with no one instance of a vicious or refractory horse in any of the teams with which we have travelled.

— *James S. Buckingham, 1838*

Yesterday morning D — and I started in a waggon and pair for the Eastern townships, the southern part of which border upon the inlet of Lake Champlain, called Missisquoi Bay.

We had heard so much of the duck-shooting on the bay that we determined to stop a day here and try our luck, so we crossed the lines and spent last night at Highgate springs in Vermont state in a large green and white hotel, fitted up for the accommodation of those who come to drink certain mineral waters of some repute in the neighbourhood. The season is over, and we occupied alone the "banquet-hall deserted." Here, though the rooms looked a little cold and empty at first, the good people soon made us very comfortable with tea and a good fire. The landlord, a thorough Yankee, received us in his bar with his feet on a high stove, his chair thrown back on its hind-legs, a cigar in his mouth, one eye shut, and his hat on. He was rather cool and contemptuous at first but softened by degrees and ended by treating us very well; so much so indeed that the next morning when we got up to go out shooting at four o'clock, though it was bitterly cold, he insisted upon getting up too and giving us our breakfast before we started.

The morning proved so stormy that the "hunters" with whom we had made an appointment could not bring over their boat, and though we paddled about for some time in two wretched little punts, about as seaworthy as a washing-tub, we got very few shots, as we were afraid to venture into deep water. The plan adopted by the hunters here is to paddle in one of these little punts, which do very well for one person through grass and reeds; and after waiting perhaps half a day they get a shot at a flock sitting and kill a dozen or more. They never shoot flying and hardly ever at a single bird, so that nothing can be more different than their idea of sport and ours. These pot-hunters express great surprise that a man who can afford to buy game should take the trouble to hunt it.

— *Joseph Robert Godley, 1842*

Flaming Maples, Chelsea, by John H. Vondell

Green River Village, Guilford, by A. C. Shelton

Birch and Cherry, below, by Ernest Gay

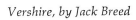
Vershire, by Jack Breed

Maple-lined Road, West Barnet, by Winston Pote

Lower Waterford Sugarhouse, by Dick Smith

Wheelock,
by Grant Heilman

The Lost Art of Sneaking

MURRAY HOYT

You have no idea how the fine Fall sport of duck hunting has deteriorated during the last six or eight decades. Why, I was actually in a *heated* duck blind last fall. Not only heated, but thermostat-regulated.

Vermont duck hunting in the old days used to demand a stoicism in the face of torture that would have made a Hindu Fakir turn pale. Today a frail little old lady, subject to colds and sinus congestion, could go duck hunting and experience practically no extra discomfort.

The old blind was made up of flat stones, or of cedars woven into a framework. The more lush numbers occasionally had a roof which even more occasionally didn't leak. Sometimes blinds were built on stilts and you reached them by boat. In a wind, water swished up through the floor with each wave. On a cold enough day your boots and the floor would coat with ice, making any movement while you had a gun in your hand about as safe as Russian roulette.

To pick up dead ducks, if any, you either had trained a dog or rowed out yourself. The dog gambit was fine once the dog's training was complete. But sometimes you or he would die of old age before you could complete it. In the meantime, with flying ducks sheering off in alarm because dead ones lay in the decoys, your black messenger was likely to sit there with his big limpid eyes looking into yours, his tail wagging, maybe offering you his paw or licking your hand. But definitely not doing any such stupid thing as going swimming in *that* water. Or if you finally got him into the water, he'd return with the nearest decoy in his mouth wearing the pleased, happy and forgiving look of one who has met with great credit the impossible demands of an unfeeling monster. And he would then shake water all over you.

So you'd row out and get the ducks yourself. And while you were out there you'd see a small flock flying close to shore, obviously intent on decoying. So you'd lie down in the bottom of the boat in the hope that you wouldn't scare them and that your pal would get a shot. And the ducks would see you and gain enough altitude so that anti-aircraft couldn't have downed them. And there'd be an inch of water in the bottom of the boat — there's *always* water in the bottom of a duck boat — which would make its clammy way through your clothing to your skin and torture you throughout the remainder of a miserably wonderful day.

Then there used to be the matter of the care and transportation of decoys. Decoys in those days were amazingly life-like birds carved lovingly from blocks of cedar during long winter evenings. Each decoy had an anchor of some sort attached to its bottom by a hunk of thin rope; for an anchor you used a big bolt or nut or mowing machine guard. You divided up your decoys into the same number of burlap bags that you had hunters, and then you carried them from the car to the duck blind.

You'd try to hold the top of the bag over your shoulder with one hand, pick up your boxes of shells, your shotgun, your spare shotgun, your lunch, the thermos jug your wife sent, maybe even one of a pair of oars, with the other. This could sometimes get out of hand, both figuratively and literally.

For the first hundred feet everything was

pretty light and manageable. Then the weight of everything would increase by a sort of horrible geometric progression.

Inanimate shotguns, oars, jugs, boxes, would suddenly come to life and begin to squirm in your arms. Even if you had only one shotgun and one oar, they would strive with all the power of a dowsing rod in sympathetic hands, to form the letter X with each other. Then mowing machine guards, bolts, duck bills, areas of the duck even further south, would begin to gouge. The pain would become excruciating. Boy, was it fun.

What happens now? They use rubber decoys and inflate them when they get to the lake. Your little niece could carry all the decoys you'd need, flat and uninflated, under one arm on a day when she wasn't actually feeling her best. I even saw one ingenious character using his golf cart to pull two shotguns and a pair of oars upright.

That, you understand, was the easy duck-blind hunting. There was also the "sneaking" of ducks. Sneaking ducks! Now there's a lost art like livery-stable-managing or street-car-conductoring. And like them, it was the victim of the gasoline engine. Because nowadays if the ordinary duck hunter can't four-wheel-drive right there, he won't go there. And he isn't going to crawl a quarter of a mile on his, if you'll pardon the expression, belly for the best duck on earth. Never.

There's plenty of walking and crawling, too. They don't put bays very close together. After you've approached one of them with the caution of a public-enemy about to peek into a State Police barrack's window, and have found it empty, you've got to walk half a mile before you can look into the *next* one. Chances are you're wearing heavy boots, long-handled underwear with patio entrance, a couple of wool shirts, and a hunting jacket to carry your shells. You're also carrying a shotgun. A big heavy shotgun. Sweat pours off you. However, if you didn't wear that much, you'd freeze to death while you were lying on the snow-covered ground later.

Let's suppose that in the fifth bay there are ducks. We'll suppose, too, (though there's no real reason we should) that when you crane your neck, they don't turn out to be right down below the bank where you hadn't expected them and where they have you in plain sight; that you don't watch them fly away while you stand there in the blue haze of brimstone, a broken and frustrated man.

We'll suppose that they're in the middle of the bay. They are diving for weed roots close to shore. Their position and the diving are, as Madison Avenue duck hunters would put it, plus factors. However, in sneaking ducks there are also minus factors. Big, juicy, garden-variety minus factors in profusion. Always. The minus factors here are that it's an open pasture with no brush, and that the whole works slopes toward the lake so that the ducks can see you and all the pasture at any time.

You work your way back, keeping whatever has been shielding you, between you and the ducks. You circle around behind the slope. Then you move forward cautiously to look over the top, down at the ducks.

Scientists say that a hawk has such terrific eyesight that he can see a mouse from an unbelievable height. Hah! I'd stack a hardened old drake whistler against six hawks anytime. Furthermore a drake whistler goes under the theory that if it wasn't there yesterday, this is no place for him.

So you surface behind some grass and an old thistle, and there are the ducks. They pop into sight one or two at a time till there are a dozen or more. Then one at a time they dive again till they're all under. You have about ten seconds between the time the last one disappears and the first ones start popping out again.

So you pick out another clump of grass and thistles maybe fifteen yards ahead. The split second the last duck goes under, you run forward, crouched over, and dive behind the new clump. You try to become part of the ground, because there's no hill to hide you now. You've either got to be mistaken for upland posies or you aren't going to eat duck.

They all go under, and you run again. Again you dive behind your pre-selected cover with a slide that would do credit to Willie Mays going into second base head first. Only Willie doesn't carry a shotgun, the barrel of which he's got to keep from plugging. And snow doesn't scoop down the front of his shirt. Did you ever lie flat on your stomach on about a quart of snow between your shirt and your birthday suit? It's an experience. Add to this the fact that you can't move a muscle, that your cheek is pressed hard against the cold, snow-covered ground, your opposite eye is watching ducks through grass blades, your clawlike hands have stiffened with cold to the point where you doubt if you could let go of the gun. This gives you some idea of the tremendous fun that sneaking ducks can be.

They pop out and dive; you run and dive. But their diving pattern gradually changes for the worse. If it changes, it's always for the worse. There now seems to be less than five seconds between the rear end of the last duck and the front end of the first. While you're still much too far from the water, the two finally overlap. Then you *are* stymied.

You decide to inch your way forward from clump to clump on that part of your anatomy which your wife has been after you to reduce, moving only when two or less ducks are in sight.

In spite of a tight belt you scoop snow in at the top of your pants, snow gets up your sleeves, thistles prick, and all the time your heart is pounding so from excitement that it shakes your whole frame and you hope the ducks think it's a diesel engine.

Immediately that you begin this new program of locomotion, a drake and a hen whistler stop diving altogether. They're not sure a clod — that's you — didn't change spots between the last time they dove and this time. They sit there and look up at you. You lie there and chatter your teeth at them. The rest of the ducks dive.

You've come this far, might as well keep on. But the inching forward has to be twice as cautious now. Finally you arrive, a physical wreck, at the top of the bank. Whistler and whistler's mother are still on guard. (You wonder if such a thought, in one who hates puns, isn't a sign you're cracking a little from the strain.)

Now comes the culmination of everything. But don't get the idea success is assured. Anything can still happen and probably will. Your legs can be too stiff to hold you, or you can fall down the bank. You can trip on a piece of driftwood on the beach and measure your length. A motorboat can round the point, or a partridge hunter can appear back at the top of the rise.

But let's say you're lucky and nothing evil happens. You wait till all but four ducks — the sentinels and two others — are under; you don't dare wait any longer. You leap up and run down the bank and across the beach to the water's edge.

Instantly the four ducks take off; there's no chance for a shot at them. Shaking with excitement and cold you throw the gun up. You point it at the spot where the rest of the ducks went under. The gun barrel, from your shaking, is making figure eights.

The ducks come up all right. From underneath they've seen the bottoms of those sentinels leave the surface. They explode out of water in full flight like Polaris missiles. And they do it everywhere except where they went under and where and when you expect them. Some come bursting out instantly. Others swim under water and then burst out far away, or to one side — any place to make it difficult.

You have just three shots. You take what you think may be the best three shots you'll get. Hitting a duck under those conditions ranks for skill right along with playing "The Flight of the Bumblebee" on the violin. After your gun is empty, two more ducks burst up right in front of you, the best shots yet.

Suppose you were successful and did kill one. How are you going to get him? There's a ridge of ice along the shore where spray has frozen. It's a cinch you aren't going to swim. And, duck sneaking being how it is, the wind is blowing *away* from shore. Always.

So you throw rocks. The idea is to land the rock just beyond the duck (but not too far beyond) so that the wash will, move the duck a few inches inshore. And believe me for this business you need to be Bob Gibson and Jim Lonborg and a few others rolled into one. You gain a foot, and then you land a rock on the wrong side of the duck and lose six inches of your gain.

So that's duck-sneaking. Understand, I've only scratched the surface on the items that can go wrong. I've had a gun jam, the first shell misfire, and an eagle come down and pick up my duck after I'd shot it, to mention only a few.

Why, in the old days you had to be a marathon runner, an Indian warrior, an acrobat, a trick shot artist and a baseball pitcher to sneak them. And you had to be several of these things as well as an arctic-survival expert to hunt them from a blind.

They just don't build duck hunters now the way they used to.

Burke Hollow, by Mack Derick

Frosty Morning, Arlington, by H. Stanley Johnson

Camel's Hump from Richmond, by Pauline Craig

The Connecticut at Wells River, by Bullaty-Lomeo

Pomfret Road, by Arthur Griffin

East Topsham, by Hans Wendler

Dead Creek, Addison, by Hanson Carroll

Camel's Hump, from Waterbury Center, by Dick Smith

Ottauquechee River, by Abner Kodess

Hazen Road, Peacham,
by Bullaty-Lomeo

Time of the Leaf Watchers

WALTER R. HARD, JR.

As long as most Vermonters can recall, Autumn has been the season not so much of the harvest as the time when the leaf watchers arrive. Most of the Fall visitors are older people, traveling with more leisure (and money) and more interest in the life around them than their frenetic Summer counterparts. This, then, as every real estate agent knows, also is the season for serious part-time, retirement or migrating home-searchers.

By the 1960s, however, the pokers along leaf-strewn back roads were finding a short supply of quaint characters on neat hill farms (these possibly for sale.) The changes already were well advanced, but how far?

Asked Ralph N. Hill in 1960: "Is Vermont, which John Gunther has written is the most impregnably Yankee of all the states, really unspoiled, or is this a myth inspired by the gospel according to fanatics? The answer is largely, yes, particularly in the north, which as Walter Hard remarked, has not yet been 'summerized.'

"In *Faces in the Crowd* David Riesman wonders if the northcountry will continue to produce such men (as once led the nation), since the younger generation stands relatively idle — without the old necessities. A majority of the trailblazers came off the farms or out of the small towns.

"The farms these days are dwindling rapidly in number. Without an avenue to the great stream of interstate commerce, the small towns are having a struggle for a place in the sun. Their people will find it hard to maintain their traditional independence if they become enmeshed in the cogs of rural suburbia; but unless they gear themselves to the complex economic apparatus of the Twentieth Century they cannot subsist. This is the problem."

Vermonters, increasingly had been migrating within the state to more urban centers of employment, and were beginning to express a dissatisfaction with the vestigal bars to natural change. Impatient newcomers grew more outspoken in their efforts to change political habit. Even earlier the old virtues had been questioned by traditionalist Dorothy Fisher:

"The Vermont scheme of life is fine for able-bodied, hard-working people sound in wind and limb and with good headpieces, but it is very hard on the sick, the old, the helplessly dependent and tragically hard on the subnormal."

Commenting on Vermont's perhaps unjustified pride in public honesty, William Allen White had observed that "there are so few nickels in Vermont, and every one is marked, that everybody in the state knows exactly where every one of them is at all times. How could anybody steal one?" Yes, Mrs. Fisher conceded: "Vermont has [*until recently perhaps*] kept its personality, just because it has not been driven to become different by industrial prosperity."

The difference really was a camouflage, suggested Chilton Williamson in the *Saturday Review.* "Vermonters were fearfully regimented for a long time by the inexorable law of comparative economic (dis)advantage."

But the era of questioning now ended. Vermont "is mentally snowed in", charged departing University of Vermont professor John W. Aldridge. The state "needs to get over its hick provincial attitude," he said, but it is "so bogged down in rural interests," that he "could not imagine for it a healthy future."

As farm life continued to decline as a dominant economic force, dissatisfaction came to center on the state's "rurally dominated legislature." Wrote Pownal transplant William J. Smith of *My Poetic Career in Vermont Politics:* "The cow has always been prominent in Vermont; and most of them vote, since our representation is, in effect, based on acreage."

While bitterness was expressed against the old survivals, scorn was leveled, too, against selfish opportunism being shown by some natives. Said John Kenneth Galbraith, a part-time resident (by his own, preferred terminology) in speaking of useful local enterprises:

"[In these] the local Vermonters do not participate to any extent. They have a strong preference for profitable activity. This means they are rarely to be found running country inns, making furniture, growing African violets (an especially imaginative current venture) or raising horses or potatoes.

"U.S. Route 5 makes its way along the eastern border of the state through a hideous neon-lighted tunnel walled by motels, antique shops, roadside furniture shops featuring not Vermont but North Carolina craftsmanship and, of course, service stations and restaurants. Quite a few local people can be found here, for they have discovered that the Humbert Humberts patronize the garish bazaars in preference to the lovely local villages, as does almost everyone else."

Miriam Chapin had even harsher words: "The collaborators, citizens who make a living out of visitors and new residents drawn by the love-liness of mountain villages . . . are the native Vermonters who seize the opportunity to drag out of their attics spinning wheels — set out the goods by the roadside and wait for the tourists. Or they sell real estate, start motels and snack bars, open filling stations.

"A very few of the native Vermonters do survive in pristine state . . . decimated, not entirely uncorrupted by civilization. They are, of course, looked down upon by the respectable, and they resent it. But in return they get a lot of amusement out of the behavior of the summer folks. 'That new fellow bought the Town Farm, he left his car out by the woods the other night, and the porcupines chewed every tire on it.' Within narrow limits, closing in each year, they preserve some freedom."

"The new Vermont offers little privacy any more. The machine age," Mrs. Chapin concluded, "has come upon it before it was ready, and the state must become used to public living and learn to regulate it. It has not yet."

The cool, New Yorker's eye of Hal Burton tried to assess things in 1961: "Like a Puritan beset by the temptations of the flesh, Vermont is painfully examining its own soul in a struggle to decide whether being the last Yankee state is worth the sacrifice it entails. The alternative is to give up its independent ways.

"Until the tourist era reached its apogee after World War II, precious few people passed through en route to points beyond. This kept Vermont a rural backwater, appealing to antiquarians but set apart spiritually from the rest of the United States. Vermont changed so little because it had no incentive to change."

Burton cited a visiting economist's judgment that "it isn't that these people are so prudent. It's simply that they are scared to bet on the future." Citing Vermont's then existing malapportioned legislature, habitual Republicanism, archaic judicial system and high suicide rate, Burton summed up that: "The legend of Vermont as a paradise on earth, is subject to some suspicion."

The Pleasures and Uses of Bankruptcy

Since the end of World War II, we have been coming to an old farm in southeastern Vermont. Once here, the days lengthen perceptibly. There is magic in the late evening mist on our meadows and the way the early morning sun comes through the maples. Life acquires a new tranquillity. So, we think, do the children. . . .

As a teacher of economics I am visited each summer by a certain number of my professional friends and colleagues. Without exception, they inquire about the economic underpinnings of this part of Vermont. I have found the line of thought which these questions set in motion to be troublesome. The hills and narrow valleys north of the Massachusetts line and between the Green Mountains and the Connecticut look reasonably prosperous but are without visible means of support. There are no important industries — fortunately. The valleys have a few dairy farms, but it is northern Vermont which fattens on the revenues and suffers the vicissitudes of the Boston milk shed. . . .

There are the part-time residents. We contribute something to the economic life but we are no gold mine.

But gradually I have become aware of another source of revenue which is important. And those who supply it add greatly to the comfort, convenience and pleasure of country life and may even make it tolerable. These are the people who systematically disburse their savings, money they have inherited or whatever they can borrow,

on enterprises conducted for the public good. They grow things, make useful articles or (most important of all) render valuable services which one could never obtain on a purely commercial basis. The prices are not always low, but since they are always well below cost no one can complain. The community benefits not only from the goods and services they supply but also from the rent or interest they pay, the purchases they make and payrolls they meet. To be sure, the day comes when the rent, interest, bills and payroll become troublesome or can no longer be met. But, invariably others come along. The competition to serve the public at a loss is rather keen. In a town not far from here is an inn which has failed decisively in the financial sense not once but twice in the past five years. It is now up for sale at the highest price yet. The chances of getting the asking price or something close to it are excellent. On the basis of this and other cases, it is my belief that service generally improves with each bankruptcy.

Inns provide the best example of capital consumption, to give this admirable phenomenon its technical name. In the course of an autumn holiday, to offer what economists call a synthetic model of reality, a man and his wife from New Canaan take a leisurely motor trip to Montreal. They are fond of the country, which is why they live in Fairfield County and why they chose this particular trip. Somewhere between Brattleboro and Montpelier they spend the night at a village inn on a secondary road — not a motel but the real thing with elms and maples all but hiding the small Shell station across the way. What peace! What a contrast between the life of the innkeepers and their own! Independence and serenity as against the daily penance on the New Haven, the obscene struggle on the subway and the crushing pressures of organization.

The travelers have talked of getting off the rat race. Could it really happen? It won't happen to many people, but it could happen to them. The husband has about fifteen years before actuarial decrepitude, the sense to know it, and a keen desire to enjoy the years that remain. His wife is younger and a good companion. They have some money. They have something even more precious, which is the imagination and courage and a knowledge of how to cook. . . .

Fortune regularly publishes vignettes of small business ingenuity, enterprise and success. Quite a number of these tell of men who have found fulfillment and success. None tells of failure. Those of us who profit from the savings of those who are going broke are profoundly indebted to these and similar success stories. . . .

The couple returns to the village and searches out the real estate man. He is not hard to find.

"Yes, there is a good small inn for sale." It turns out to be the one at which they stopped. This is no coincidence; nearly all small country inns are for sale. Being from New York and therefore experienced in the tools of modern management, the husband has a good hard look at the books. He finds that it has been losing money. Perceptively and quite correctly, he attributes the losses to bad management. What he does not know is that such enterprises never make enough money to give the impression even of indifferent management.

So the previous owners go back to New Jersey. For four years, they have furnished jobs and modest wages to the community. They have bought meat and frozen vegetables from the local grocer and quite a lot of liquor from the state store. There were moments when it seemed possible that the liquor might put them back in the black and other less commercial interludes when it eased toil and softened anxiety. The part-time residents have had a place with atmosphere and home cooking at which to dine and, on occasion, to deposit a redundant guest. During the two-week deer season and week before Labor Day, business was always amazing — several times what could be accommodated. The total cost of so benefiting the community was $13,600. It would have been more, but, because of the competition to serve, they are selling out at a considerable capital gain. They have also provided us with considerable unpaid labor, although it is the capital that really counts.

The future is also bright. The local carpenter and his two men can look forward to the busiest autumn since

the other couple from New Jersey converted the barn into a full-time furniture factory. For the new owners of the inn have unhesitatingly identified better management with modernizing the kitchen, refurnishing the bedrooms, adding two baths and making the former woodshed into a cozy new bar. These improvements will make the inn a better place to leave or take guests and more of an all-round community asset.

Lest anyone think this story is contrived, let me return to strict matters of experience. For years, we have been eating meals at a succession of inns that were being endowed by their owners. The owners were from the city. All were able to bring a modest amount of capital to our service. We always guessed that they were spending money on us and this could have meant — there are some subtle differences here between average and marginal costs — that each visit absorbed some of their capital. Nonetheless, we always felt that our patronage was a real favor and so did they. We were always sorry to see them go, as eventually they did, but we were comforted by the knowledge that others would take their place, and others always have.

As a nation, we owe much to subsidies. . . . Evidently, therefore, we need feel no shame that our pleasant countryside is subsidized by aspiring small enterprisers. And as subsidies go, this is an excellent one. Unlike the depletion allowances enjoyed by the oilmen, it brings no complaints, quite justified, of fantastic favoritism. Our subsidy is perfectly reliable, for as I have noted, when one entrepreneur has exhausted his capital and credit, another is always ready and eager to take his place. The very best journals proclaim the virtue of such sacrifice on our behalf. It is a demonstration of worth, an affirmation of faith in the system. A recession or depression would, one imagines, increase the number of people seeking the serenity of the country and the security of their own businesses. The outlays must have a certain cogency to the individuals involved, but this has nothing to do with the great impersonal sweep of economic forces.

— *John Kenneth Galbraith*

winter

Peacham Storm, by Carsten W. Johnson

East Corinth, by E. L. Gockeler

Woodstock Sleigh-ride, by David Lawlor

Snow-capped Jay Peak, by VDD

Mt. Equinox from Bromley Mountain, by Bullaty-Lomeo

Missisquoi Valley Sunset, by Grant Heilman

West Dover Road, by Rod Allin

Passumpsic River Mist, by Dick Smith

Norwich Sunset, by Hanson Carroll

Frosty Elm, Thetford, by Gladys W. Estabrook

View near Waitsfield, by Ozzie Sweet

Winter Woods,
by Hanson Carroll

Sufferings and Settlements

RALPH N. HILL

In the latter part of February I set out from the town of Norwalk, in Connecticut, on my journey for Wolcott to commence a settlement and make that my residence; my family consisting of my wife and five children, they all being girls, the eldest nine or ten years old. My team was a yoke of oxen and a horse. After I had proceeded on my journey to within about one hundred miles of Wolcott one of my oxen failed, but I kept him yoked with the other till about noon each day, then took his end of the yoke myself and proceeded on in that manner with my load to about fourteen miles of my journey's end, when I could get the sick ox no further, and was forced to leave him with Thomas W. Connel in Johnson; but he had neither hay nor grain for him.

I then proceeded to Hydepark: this brought me to about eight miles of Wolcott and to the end of the road. It was now about the 20th of March; the snow not far from four feet deep; no hay to be had for my team and no way for them to subsist but by browse. As my sick ox at McConnel's could not be kept on browse I interceded with a man in Cambridge for a little hay to keep him alive, which I backed, a bundle at a time, five miles, for about ten days, when the ox died.

We were the first families in Wolcott: in Hydepark there had two families wintered the year before. To the east of us it was eighteen miles to inhabitants and no road but marked trees: to the south, about twenty, where there was infant settlements but no communication with us; and to the north it was almost indefinite, or to the regions of Canada. I had now got to the end of my journey and I may say almost to the end of my property, for I had not a mouthful of meat or kernel of grain for my family, nor had I a cent of money left to buy with, or property that I could apply to that purpose. I however had the good luck to catch a sable. The skin I carried fifty miles and exchanged for half a bushel of wheat, and backed it home. We had now lived three weeks without bread, though I had bought a moose of an Indian and backed the meat five miles, which answered to subsist upon.

When I came into Wolcott my farming tools consisted of one axe and an old hoe. The first year I cleared about two acres wholly without any team, and being short of provision was obliged to work till harvest with scarce a sufficiency to support nature. My work was chiefly by the river. When too faint to labour, for want of food, I used to take a fish from the river, broil it on the coals and eat it without bread or salt, and then to my work again.

I had the good fortune to buy on trust the [second] winter, of a man in Cambridge twenty-four miles from home, twelve bushels of corn and one of wheat. The man was so good as to take his team and carry it to the mill. The owner of the mill asked me how I expected to get my meal home. I answered him that I knew not. The feeling man then offered me his oxen and sled, and turned to the miller and directed him to grind my grist toll free. While at the mill a man requested me to bring a half hogshead tub on my sled up to Johnson. By permission of the owner of the oxen he put the tub on the sled, and it was a Providential circumstance, for when I came to Brewster's branch, a wild stream,

I found it broken up, run rapid and deep. At first I was perplexed what to do. To go across with my bags on the sled would ruin my meal; I soon thought of the tub; this held about half my bags; the other half I left on the shore, and proceeded into the branch and crossed with safety. Though I was wet nearly to my middle, I unloaded the tub and returned into the branch, holding the tub on the sled, but the stream was so rapid, the tub being empty, that in spite of all my exertions I was washed off the sled and carried down stream, holding on to the tub. At length I succeeded in getting the tub to the shore, though I was washed off the sled and carried down the stream more than twenty rods, sometimes up to my armpits, and how I kept the tub from filling in I know not, but so it was. I then put in the other half of my load and succeeded in getting the whole across the branch, and travelled on about three miles and put up for the night.

In the morning I proceeded for home — came to the [Lamoille] river; not being sensible how weak the ice was, I attempted to cross, but here a scene ensued that I can never forget. When about half across the river I perceived the ice settling under my oxen. I jumped on to the tongue of my sled, and hastened to the oxen's heads and pulled out the pin that held the yoke. By this time the oxen were sunk to their knees in water. I then sprang to the sled and drawed it back to the shore without the least difficulty, notwithstanding the load, and returned to my oxen. By this time they had broken a considerable path in the ice and were struggling to get out. I could do nothing but stand and see them swim around — sometimes they would be nearly out of sight, nothing scarcely but their horns to be seen — they would then rise and struggle to extricate themselves from their perilous situation. I called for help in vain; and to fly for assistance would have been imprudent and fatal.

At length the oxen swam up to where I stood and laid their heads on the ice at my feet. I immediately took the yoke from off their necks; they lay still till the act was performed and then returned to swimming as before. By this time they had made an opening in the ice as much as two rods across. One of them finally swam to the down stream side and in an instant, as if lifted out of the water, he was on his side on the ice, and got up and walked off; the other swam to the same place and was out in the same way. I stood on the opposite side of the opening and saw with astonishment every movement. I then thought, and the impression is still on my mind, that they were helped out by supernatural means; most certainly no natural cause could produce an effect like this: that a heavy ox six and a half feet in girth can of his own natural strength heave himself out of the water on his side on the ice, is too extraordinary to reconcile to a natural cause; — that in the course of Divine Providence events do take place out of the common course of nature, that our strongest reasoning cannot comprehend, is impious to deny: though we acknowledge the many chimeras of superstition, ignorance and barbarism in the world; and when we are eye witnesses to such events, it is not for us to doubt, but to believe and tremble.

— *Seth Hubbell, 1789*

I asked him if he would give me a ride to Windsor, or part of the way. He said his load was heavy but he could carry my pack, and I might take hold of the hind part of the sleigh and ride down hill, if I could keep up so. This he thought was impossible for me to do. I told him I was used to walking and running, and could keep up. We set out early in the morning, and he having two good horses, sometimes drove faster than I wished him to go. When going down the hills he would say, "you will kill yourself in running so long and fast." We arrived at Windsor about four o'clock; there he stopped and gave me my pack. I was then about thirteen or fourteen miles from my father's house and was determined to get there before I slept.

After walking about three miles I came to an house where a baptist deacon lived, by the name of Thompson. When I took off my shoes my stockings were quite bloody, my feet having been so wet all day and stepping so hard in keeping up with the sleigh. After eating some food and resting a little I set out about sundown for Woodstock. My limbs were so sore that sometimes it appeared impossible for me to reach home that night. I walked very slow all the way, and some time between midnight and day I arrived at my father's house, almost overcome. When I opened the door my mother sat by the fire, having two beds in the room; on one lay my oldest brother, on the other my youngest sister, sick with the measles.

After I had retired to sleep my mother took my stockings and put them into water to wring them out; and she told me the next day that the water was red with the blood she wrung out of them. My feet were very sore for several days after, and to add to all the rest, I took the measles and was not able to do much for about one month after my return.

— *Elias Smith, 1789*

Daniel Hall had a grant of a hundred acres in St. Johnsbury, but had not received the deed from a Dr. Arnold, who had died. From the doctor's son Hall received instead a hundred acres "up in Lyndon". His activities were described to Edward T. Fairbanks as follows:

Hall satisfied — next morning up early — packs wife and goods on hand sled—travels to Lyndon — on crust — unpacks wife and goods — builds fire — sets up Wigwam — moves in wife and goods — all settled — sundown. Next morning nothing to eat — takes gun — sallies into forest — tracks a moose — big one — shoots moose — skins thigh — cuts out steak — carries home — wife delighted — roasts meat on forked stick — after breakfast calls up all neighbors — they skin moose — each takes a piece — Hall gets out hand sled — loads on moose meat and pelt — goes to St. Johnsbury — trades — gets three pecks potatoes, half bushel meal, peck salt — carries home to wife — wife delighted — sundown.

— *1793*

At Whitehall we embarked in sleighs on Lake Champlain; the afternoon was bright and mild, and well disposed us to enjoy the pleasing change from our snailpaced waggon to the smooth rapidity of a sleigh, gliding at the rate of nine mile an hour. The first object our driver was happy to point out to us was several of our own flotilla [the British fleet from the Battle of Plattsburg] anchored near the town, sad "trophies of the fight".

At Shoreham, nearly opposite to Crown Point, we found good accommodation for the night at Mr. Larenburg's tavern, and set off the next morning before breakfast; but we had soon cause to repent of thus committing ourselves to the mercy of the elements. The lake now began to widen, and the shores to sink in the same proportion; the keen blasts of the north, sweeping over its frozen expanse, pierced us with needles of ice; the thermometer was 22° below zero; buffalo hides, bear skins, caps, shawls and handkerchiefs were vainly employed against a degree of cold so much beyond our habits. Our guide, alone of the party, his chin and eyelashes gemmed and powdered with the drifting snow, boldly set his face and his horses in the teeth of the storm. Sometimes a crack in the ice would compel us to wait, while he went forward to explore it with his axe (without which the American sleigh-drivers seldom travel) when, having ascertained its breadth and the foothold on either side, he would drive his horses at speed and clear the fissure, with its snow ridge, at a flying leap; a sensation we found agreeable enough, but not so agreeable as a good inn and dinner at Burlington.

— *Francis Hall, 1816*

Near Pawlet,
by E. L. Gockeler

East Burke, by Winston Pote

Prosper, by Frank Lieberman

Mt. Mansfield, by Arthur Griffin

Barnet Center,
by Carsten W. Johnson

Tobogganing,
by Ernest Gay

Woodstock Farm, left, by Ruth Archer

Waterbury Center, by Pauline Craig

Blizzard, Hartford,
by Hanson Carroll

On Enjoying the Cold

MURRAY HOYT

Vermont farmers, back each side of the turn of the century, loved a good blizzard.

Oh, I realize that all farmers will deny this fact indignantly. Love a blizzard? How absurb can you get? Think of the work. The shoveling; the hardships; the destruction; the disruption of travel. Love it indeed! They hated it just like all farmers always have and always will.

Okay, I hear you; just the same they loved it. What's more, present-day Vermont farmers do too, though to a lesser degree.

Sure a blizzard is powerful, destructive, makes work. It's awe-inspiring in its power. Anne Bosworth Greene has described a Vermont country blizzard's beginnings far better than I could. She says, "A storm is sweeping across the hills. From a soft blue the sky grew swiftly gray, and I looked out in time to see Long Hill losing itself in whiteness. In the valley gray veils began whirling against the woods; and there the storm seemed to stay. But it must have been racing towards us, for in another instant great flakes came against our big elms, at first indefinitely, them making a fierce rush up the hill. Recruits joined them, the valley thickened, and now I can see only the line of trees by the first wall — thin, ghostly in the driving snow. It pours down in blinding floods between my window and the orchard. . . . The wind roars; there are rattlings and shiverings. . . . The storm is howling outside, the wind tearing at the building, shaking it."

A menacing, frightening thing, such a storm. Yet Mrs. Greene, who must have experienced many blizzards, says, "I love this blotting out of the storm. One feels so sheltered, so wrapped around."

That's the whole thing in a nutshell. That's the feeling the farmer gets. And it's one of the most pleasant, most primitive feelings in the world. The storm howls outside. But inside he is safe. There is warmth that he can draw around him, there is light. Each blast of the wind accentuates the difference between outside and in. Perhaps there's a fireplace, perhaps there's a huge kitchen range. Either way there will be the pleasant crackling of burning wood. The cat dozes on the hearth, or on a rocking chair beside the range. The dog, his jowls on his front paws, one eye cocked, lies just out from under foot but nicely within range of the direct warmth. The farmer knows that in the barn his cows and horses munch the hay he has lately thrown down for them. There will be the soft stomping, the rattling of stanchions, the other small noises of their presence. The barn, too, is sheltered and warm, kept so by the body heat of so many animals together. The cat purrs loudly and the farmer knows for once exactly how she feels. If it were seemly in a man, he wouldn't mind purring himself.

The windows steam up from the supper-getting. The howling goes on. The supper is put upon the table. There are platters and serving dishes piled high with meat, potatoes, vegetables from the vegetable cellar below them or from the cold cellar where the hundreds of cans of eatables that were filled last summer, sit in long neat rows. There's a huge pitcher of milk. The family eats, a little subdued this evening by the presence and wild sounds of the storm outside.

The storm grows wilder. From time to time

during the evening the farmer rises from his easy chair, goes to the window. A drift where the wind eddies back against the house, has reached the sill now, will probably go halfway up the window. Flakes swirl within the window's light. The night is a vast black nothing outside that pitifully small patch of window light. The storm howls on.

The farmer looks at his family, the children studying, his wife reading in the comfort and warmth which he has provided them. And that wonderful feeling of being "sheltered, wrapped around" grows inside him until it produces a contentment mixed with pride that he wouldn't trade for any other feeling in the world right at that moment.

Because this is the culmination of all his planning, of all his work, of all his family's labor. He has known, oh so surely, that this night would come. It always comes in Vermont sometime during the winter. Laboriously he has prepared for it. And now they are tested, and he and his family and his animals are warm and dry and safe.

Perhaps he puts on his winter clothes and wades out to the barn before he goes to bed. Ostensibly this is to see if the stock are all right, but really it is to savor that nice feeling further. He looks in lantern light at the hay in the wide, dark mows overhead in the cowbarn (and acting as insulation above his cattle). He stands there and savors it, all that work, all those hours, days, months, getting ready. And it was enough and good. If he lives along the east border of the state he may even own one of those New Hampshire-type houses with the buildings all strung together so that he doesn't have to wade at all, just passes through building after building to the cowbarn.

Sure, he'll have to shovel in the morning. But the exercise might even be good for him in winter. He'll talk about the blizzard and protest to passing neighbors, after the roads are "broken out", how horrible it was and how he hated it. And he'll wear a cat-that-ate-the-canary smile. They, too, will protest their hate for it, and they, too, will have a pleased, excited tone in their voices as they tell about this road blocked, or that-sized drift in the hollow.

Travel disruption? The farmer in those days wasn't going anywhere anyhow. There were no cars, and thus no commitments for meetings in town. He didn't have to drive his son to the basketball game. Or listen to the griping of his offspring if there was a dance the storm kept them from attending. In the old days if the farm's young people went on to high school, they boarded in town from Monday to Friday, and getting to school events was their problem. He didn't have to find a way to get his wife to the Woman's Club meeting in the face of the storm.

Admittedly, things are different today. Pole barns aren't even warm. But sometimes, when the storm is so bad that going anywhere is out of the question, I think that today's Vermont farmer deep inside enjoys that lovely feeling as much as his grandfather did.

But like him, he'd never admit it. Not on your tintype.

The turn-of-the-century Vermonter who lived on the western side of our state, very often went fishing in mid-winter when the snow was too deep for outside work. He fished even in below zero weather in his shirt sleeves, comfortable and cozy and warm. He did it inside a small house. He cooked and ate and slept and lived there in that house.

This is called shanty fishing. Shanty fishing for smelt today remains basically what it was in my father's day, and in his father's day. But now people come from many miles away by auto for the day's fishing, and drive home again at night (over roads kept bare with salt) instead of staying for days right in the shanties.

In the late 1800s my father, during an Easter vacation from Middlebury College, one year drove in a horse-drawn sleigh to a Lake Champlain farm whose owner had been storing the Hoyt fish shanty in a wooded gully next to the lake.

The farmer, for a fee, would also stable my father's horse with his own horses, and feed it during the week that my father planned to stay out on the ice. The shanty, like all fish shanties, was supplied with runners, like a sled. It was built of the lightest possible materials. Four square holes had been cut in the floor and replaceable covers for these had been made of the material that had been cut away.

My father and a friend who was to fish with him, dragged the shanty out across the ice to the "drop-off" where there were dozens of other shanties. They chiseled four holes in the ice that corresponded to the ones in the floor, and immediately they were in business.

The shanty was six feet by six feet. There were a couple of board seats built into two opposite walls. There was storage space under these seats. The shanty door was in the middle of a third wall, and next to the fourth wall was a small wood-burning stove complete with flat top for cooking.

On the inside face of the door had been hinged a table with a leg that let down on hinges too. This could be lowered between the two men to eat on when they sat on the two seats.

Two bunks had been hinged into opposite walls. These could be let down above the seats at night for sleeping, and folded up out of the way so that the seats could be occupied in the daytime. It was a very neat and cozy set-up.

The fish lines they hung from nails in the wall, let down through the holes to the right depth for smelt. They baited with a thin slab sliced from the side of a smelt. The baits were one and a half inches in length and a quarter of an inch in width. The hook was run through one end of this slab. With a line in each hand the fishermen "jigged" the lines (moved them up and down) and the bait darted out and in, out and in, and looked like a small minnow.

The fish started to bite rapidly that day. When one of them bit, the man who had the bite would drop his other line — it was still attached to the nail so that there was no chance of his losing it — and pull his fish in hand over hand. If the bait was still fresh looking, he would drop it back into the water. And while it was sinking, he would grab and try the line he had abandoned. If he felt a fish on it, in turn, he'd continue hauling till it, too, came up through the hole.

The little stove heated the shanty quickly to a comfortable temperature for shirt-sleeve fishing, and they closed off the draft. Smelt mounted in the pail quite rapidly. When my father and his friend hung coats over the small windows of the shanty, to shut out light, they could see their baits plainly, dangling down below them. Around the baits at all times swam a dozen or more of the small, almost transparent, hard-to-see smelt, ghosting slowly in and out of sight. Often one of them grabbed the bait, more often they just swam slowly past. Once in a while one would charge in and crash into the sinker for no apparent reason. After he'd done this he'd sort of reel off away from there like a fighter who has barely weathered the round and is trying to find his corner after the bell. I've heard a man laugh right out loud, up above in his shanty, when he watched this byplay.

At noon they pan-fried some of the smelt they had caught, along with a little bacon. Any fish under eight inches in length they picked up by the tail and ate bones and all. Cooking softens the bones of smelt, which it definitely doesn't do for most other fish, till you scarcely know you're eating them.

The work sleigh from Port Henry, New York, drawn by a team of horses, arrived at their shanty-colony while they were finishing dish washing. (The water they dipped out of the smelt holes and heated on the stove.) This was a social event. The driver bought the fish they had caught for 25¢ a pound, a very, very good price in those days, and credited the amount against the groceries that they ordered. These he would bring with him on his next day's round of the many shanty-colonies. The fish were weighed in pails on old-fashioned steelyards.

That evening after supper the two young men read a little by lantern light, let down their bunks and went to bed. They had small hard-wood chunks for the over-night fire, and when one of them woke, he would check the fire, add wood if it was needed. All night long there were rifle-like reports as the ice under them "made". These loud sharp cracks will frighten anyone who has never heard them before, but they indicate freezing, not thawing.

Life settled into a very pleasant routine. They fished, chatted with and got to know their neighbors. One day the smelt bit so avidly that they switched to pieces of red flannel for baits, and these the fish attacked without noticeable let-up.

That week of their vacation passed delightfully. All too soon they had to pack, reclaim their horse and sleigh and leave. My father said that often when they were in the dormitory studying they would think of the small ice-based village, the smell of wood smoke, the close bright stars at night, the white expanse of snow-covered ice, the coziness of their small temporary home. It would bring a nostalgic feeling of longing.

They remembered that week quite vividly all the rest of their lives.

East Jamaica, by John Harris

*Snow covered Branches, Reading, and
a Rosy Glow near Weathersfield, by Robert Holland*

Wind-swept Field, Hartford, by Hanson Carroll

Skating, Brattleboro, by Ernest Gay

Near Weston, by Bullaty-Lomeo

South Pomfret,
by David Lawlor

Ski Trail at Killington, by Hanson Carroll

At Cambridge, by Winston Pote

Shall Her Mountains Die?

WALTER R. HARD, JR.

In the Winter of 1965, influenced by a measure of outside suggestion in the form of the U.S. Supreme Court, Vermont finally re-apportioned its Legislature. By this one act the long, schizophrenic struggle between rural and urban thinking was largely remedied. As former Senator Ralph E. Flanders had written of Vermont's trauma in the late 1700s, "As a native of Vermont I have, in the background of my state's history, a case in which sovereignty was relinquished. Vermont was one of only two states which were independent nations before joining the Union. The instinct is strong to resist any demand that we give up any part of our sovereignty. We should not give it up carelessly. Only when and to the extent that it serves the national (*or local*) interest should we ever consent."

But what now was the status of Vermont's *physical* self? The early tourists to *Unspoiled Vermont* "did their full share of spoiling; the village industrialists, engineers [and] promoters have done theirs in the line of duty," wrote Storrs Lee just before the 1960s. But he optimistically felt that "Vermont can take it, for the verdure of the Green Mountains is as durable as the obsessions and idiosyncracies of the men of those mountains."

As then-Governor Philip H. Hoff said in 1967, however, to the newly apportioned Legislature: "Vermont has historically been a byway, politically as well as geographically. This is no longer true. And, despite our respect for the past, we cannot act as though it is still true. Each day we are more and more threatened by the ever sprawling cities and suburbs to the north and south of us. Our lakes, rivers and streams are increasingly objects of new exploitation. Full recognition of the pressures of this population surge must be incorporated in our attack on the problems of Vermont today and for the future."

The following year this assessment came from Samuel R. Ogden, a Vermonter by choice for the past forty years: "Vermont remains relatively unspoiled, and, as of the moment, none but the most implacable of reactionaries will insist that the old girl has been ruined.

"But how long can we proceed along these easy ways before we *do* become ruined? Many of our mountain peaks are now scarred with the worm-tracks of ski trails — white in winter and pale green in summer. New highways are being blasted through the hills, pre-empting fertile fields and the homes of men; and commercial ventures are springing up without regard for what might be proper design or fitting location or even for economic feasibility."

Ogden cited "the proliferation of road signs, the disregard for beauty on the part of highway engineers, the eyesores of public dumps and auto graveyards, the pollution of our streams and the ravishment of wild areas." Then he said: "Let's assume that, with intelligent zoning ordinances and billboard and junk and pollution control, we achieve the desired results. Our Vermont remains a green and refreshing oasis in the midst of a desert of ugliness and anxiety. But can such a condition endure? Some insist that the poisonous breath of the clanking monster is being wafted to our nostrils at this very moment. We may still have time, but I'm afraid that the thing which Vermont represents to many a badgered human is a state of being

North Windham, by John Harris

/ 149

which already has been rejected by deliberate decision of mankind.

"My point is that we Vermonters should take our beatitude as a right," Ogden concludes, "not to apologize for protecting it. We should place in chancery those of our citizens who would prostitute any of her beauty and serenity, and cause outsiders to envy and imitate us."

Vermont summer resident Wallace Stegner, citing the horrific despoiling of America's resources, asks: "And what has all this to do with Vermont, this green sanctuary of peaceful meadows and painted woods, off the main line of Progress which has swept most of the other states like a fire? I will tell you what you already know. It is coming here and you can't escape it. Vermont will have its turn after a long quiet sleep, and if a summer visitor can read the signs at all, it is in real danger of succumbing, as other regions have done, to the temptations of the boom psychology. Vermont is a little like the ocean waters along the continental shelf — hitherto safe, now threatened, but with a chance of salvation if it can organize itself to act ahead of, rather than behind, the boom.

"Failure to control the forces that would 'develop' Vermont for the tourist trade would be equivalent to letting farmers sell off their topsoil by the truckload. Beauty, like timber or grass, is a resource, subject to abuse and to the quick-profit raid, to disruption and depletion. If Vermonters can rise above their historical conservatism, which means also above their traditional individualism that sometimes approaches mule-headedness, and also above their Yankee appreciation of an immediate profit, they may

yet save this corner of the continent green and lovely."

"There are about as many signs that the north country may not be able to keep the faith, as there are that it can and will," writes Ralph N. Hill. "Certainly it cannot and should not remain in a state of nature, but it can and should use every stratagem to resist the pressures that war against its physical beauty and the individuality of its people.

"Meanwhile, it is well to repeat the prayer ascribed to the Rev. Samuel Peters, who, long before the Revolution, as he looked over a vast primeval landscape, declared: *We have met here to dedicate and consecrate this extensive wilderness and give it a new name, which new name is Verd-Mont in token that her mountains and hills shall be ever green and shall never die!"*

The Sunday Afternoon Fox

In the winter when the sun shines on the frozen lake and lights the ridge of mountains beyond, a red fox sometimes trots across the shoreline in front of my house. He does not come often; he is, I think, a solid citizen who on a particularly fine Sunday extends his afternoon walk a bit before going home to read *The New York Times* magazine section.

This fox has cost me a great deal of money, and more emotional wear and tear than a man who must budget his stability (so much for taxes, so much for home improvement) can afford. Although he does not come often, he times his entrances well. The first time I saw him was on a day three years ago when I hiked through a quarter mile of deep snow to see a patch of Vermont lakeshore I had no intention of buying. There he was, lightfooting past the spot on the shore where the real-estate promoter had just, with a wave of his arm, built a fine boathouse for the cabin cruiser I did not and do not own. At first my eyes, not myopic but city-worn, caught only the blur of color and the shape of the great, floating tail. I took him for a collie; I was not expecting a fox.

It took me only a moment to realize my mistake, and to say "fox", casually and knowledgeably. I have wondered since whether this, too, might not have been a mistake. Could the small red animal have been one of the real-estate promoter's children, zipped into a furry suit and sent scuttling across the shoreline on cue? I like to think not. But when it is midnight, with the temperature at 34 degrees below zero, and I am crawling through the crawl space beneath my house to warm the frozen plumbing with the heat of my body (as, oftener than seems possible, I am), a bitter vision obsesses me. It is a picture of the real-estate promoter doing his accounts (for the Internal Revenue Service, or for the devil) and writing down, "rental, one fox suit, $3," and "wages, one boy, 50c."

The fox settled things, of course. I pointed to him, and the promoter said, "A-yup." You don't hear many a-yups anymore, unless Vermonters are telling Vermont jokes or showing off for the summer people, but this was a beauty, one part "durned-things-are-always-under-foot," and one part "what-do-you-New-York-City-people-expect-in-Vermont — taxicabs?" The a-yup used as a sales weapon is devastating, and I was already unsettled. Trying to be agreeable on our mush through the woods, I had said of a tree, "Nice birch."

"Popple," the promoter had said, looking at me glumly. I was shaken. When the fox came along, I signed.

I remember thinking as I sank into a trance that there were no foxes in Rockefeller Center, where I then was working. This seemed at the time an unanswerable reason for buying the property. It is equally true, on reflection, that there are no armadillos in Rockefeller Center. The lack did not occur to me then, probably because I have no liking for armadillos — really, no feeling one way or the other about them. But — and this is the interesting part — I have no feeling one way or

the other about foxes either. My wife thinks this is fascinating, and I do too.

At any rate, when the seizure passed, I had in my hand the deed to half an acre of moist, low-lying shoreline (very low-lying, very moist; someone spilled a package of brown rice at a cookout last summer, and it grew). The collapse of my resistance did not seem to please the promoter. Still gloomy, he said, "I suppose you'll be wanting a camp."

As a matter of fact, I did not want a camp. A camp is a place for small boys in the summertime. If I wanted anything, it was a weekend house, and 15 minutes earlier I had not wanted that. "You mean build a house," I said.

"A camp," the promoter said. I have learned since that it is not possible to build a house on the shore of a Vermont lake. Five miles away, overtown on Main or Pleasant Street, the structure for which you bleed mortgage money would be a house. But if you can tie a boat in front of it, your castle is a camp (unless it is a "place"; places have eight bedrooms, not counting servants' quarters). Women who move to Vermont from Away find this especially hard to understand. One of them I know weeps to herself softly late at night, saying over and over again, "It's not a camp — we have a rosewood-veneer Danish sideboard."

The rosewood, the weeping and the guests came later. At first everything was joy, unpainted pine boards and guests. "We don't have much money," I told the promoter. He did not bother to a-yup this time. He had our lot, and no one was in a better position to know that we did not have much money. He decided that he would build a shell. This is a house, or camp, having, like a stuffed moose, a presentable exterior and very little except shavings inside. The shell would be ready by the first of June, he said. The mighty earthmovers, the giant cranes and the trusty artisans would commence as soon as the first violet thrust through the snow.

Time passed. It was the middle of August before the camp was abandoned — it is not proper to use the word "finished" in reference to a shell house — by the workmen. I did not realize it then, but the promoter had performed prodigies in whipping the builders to such speed. Vermont workers are bluff, honest, God-fearing, calloused philosophers who can light a kitchen match with a full swing of a double-bitted ax, but the quality for which they are most justly famed is their complete unreliability. If six men are supposed to be at work on a job, two will show up. One of these will have a sore back, and the other will have to go home again to get his tools.

If a boss carpenter has been persuaded to start work with his crew, he must be watched like a two-year-old at the beach. If he wanders off, he must be fetched back. Sometimes he will have wandered to the Folly View Diner, and here the householder's job is relatively easy. The carpenter is greeted casually and as if by accident. The householder buys him coffee and pie with ice cream. He chats for a while. Then he offers the carpenter a lift back to his house. The carpenter says no, he has his own car. This is the critical moment; the householder must be prepared to say, "Fine, I'll ride with you." This means he must leave his own car at the Folly View, and later walk back six miles to get it. It also means that if the carpenter escapes a second time, the game is lost. It is very hard to track a full-grown carpenter on foot.

The same stalking pattern is employed if the carpenter has wandered to another job (generally he will have three or four stagnating), but the hunt is made more difficult by the fact that another householder will be on hand, determined to foil any attempts to recapture the carpenter. Here the first householder must approach by stealth and appeal to the carpenter's better nature. "Looks like an emergency," the first householder says. "My job can wait; Smith will be mad as hops if you leave him with half his roof off." More times than not this will bring the carpenter; he likes the idea of Smith's ears turning red.

It should be added that none of this works with plumbers. Vermont plumbers promise, but they do not plumb. Calvin Coolidge himself could not get a faucet fixed using local labor.

For all of this, the carpenters eventually were netted,

the plumbing was improvised, and our shell, finally, was ready for gracious living. My wife and I decided to invite some friends to drive up with us for a housewarming.

It was 393 miles from midtown Manhattan to the cement block we used for a doorstep, and if you drove like Fangio you could make the distance in seven and three-quarters hours. As we left that Friday after work, our friends chatted gaily about the problems of owning a country place. Theirs was an 18th-century Connecticut farmhouse with three fireplaces, handmade nails signed by Paul Revere, and a wide-board floor in the conversation pit. Oh, the stories they had to tell about the *priceless* local couple who cooked and caretook for them! I spoke in praise of foxes. We pulled in at 3:30 a.m.

The ground was muddy, the building was dark, and the door was guarded by a pile of scrap two-by-fours and sections of electrical conduit. Our guests, Scotch-grain brogues after Italian hemp sandals, picked their way through the mulch. Inside, the female guest looked around a little desperately and then ran, Pucci-Pucci, over to one of the four collapsible aluminum chairs we had bought at the hardware store the weekend before, and which, with two studio couches, constituted the furniture. "See, Brock," she said, "Aren't these cute?" No one said anything. After a while I pointed to the floor, which was made of large pieces of plywood. "Look, wide boards," I said. No one said anything. The next morning the plumbing did not work and the fox did not show up.

Oliver Wendell Holmes was right about shells. Build thee more stately mansions next time, O my Soul, and make sure the drains work and the foxes run on time.

All of this was three years ago. Somewhat later we moved the household to Vermont. Within a week I cut my foot with an ax. The doctor said "a-yup," and a few days later I took the shoe I had been wearing to a cobbler, who said "a-yup." Later, before Christmas, I hiked into my woodlot to cut a spruce. I learned that in order to get a whack at the trunk you must lie on your side in the snow, and that when you do this, the cold water that has accumulated in your L. L. Bean gum boots trickles up your pantlegs. Lessons of this kind, well learned, offer an explanation of an aspect of the knotty Vermont character not visible in Grandma Moses Christmas cards: specifically, why so many Vermonters disappear into the root cellar with a jug for short periods, such as from November to May.

Our house is still a camp, Danish sideboard notwithstanding, but it is no longer a shell. Its walls are plastered and many of its window frames are painted. There is a lawn now, and a racketing toy tractor to cut it, and a pile of slate steppingstones beside six feet of unfinished garden-magazine slate walk. The mountains still stand on the far shore, but they are no longer part of a distant dream. Now it is New York City from which — usually when Vermont is mired in the spring mud season — Lorelei sometimes wave their handkerchiefs.

I am not going to finish the slate walk. Two weeks ago we called a trucking company, and in a few days, in one of those odd, tidal shifts that families make for no expressible reasons of necessity or desire, we are moving to New Hampshire. I say something about better schools when my friends ask me why we are going. This is not really the truth, but it would be ridiculous to say that we are going because the clatter from my house and the camps that have grown up around it has driven away the fox.

For the clatter is really in the mind, and that, perhaps, is where the fox has always been. The other day just before dusk I showed our camp to a man who wanted to rent it. "Look, you have a crane," he said. And sure enough, we did, although I had not seen it before. It was an enormous bird with great, slow wings, and it beat mockingly across the marsh and out of sight.

— *John Skow*

At Danville, by Winston Pote

Cross-country Skiing, Hartford, by Hanson Carroll

Mt. Mansfield Nose Dive, by VDD

Snowball Fight, West Brattleboro, by Ernest Gay

Bibliographies

All to the Borders (pp. 17-20)

Dutcher, L. L. "June Training in Vermont," *The Vermont Historical Gazetteer, Vol. II*, pp. 347-351. A. M. Hemenway, Burlington: 1871.

Dwight, Timothy. *Travels in New England and New York, Vol. II*. New Haven: Timothy Dwight, 1821.

Graham, John A. *A Descriptive Sketch of the Present State of Vermont*. London: Henry Fry, The Cicero Press, 1797.

Perkins, Nathan. *A Narrative of a Tour Through the State of Vermont from April 27 to June 12, 1789*. Rutland: Charles E. Tuttle Co., 1964.

Whittier, John Greenleaf. *The Song of the Vermonters 1779*. Boston: Houghton Mifflin Co., 1874.

Opening Day Ritual (pp. 29-32)

Hoyt, Murray. *The Fish in My Life*. New York: Crown Publishers, Inc., 1964.

You Are the Guardians (pp. 41-44)

Aiken, George D. *Speaking from Vermont*. New York: Stokes, 1930.

Coates, J. Walter. Cited by Ralph N. Hill in *Contrary Country*. New York: Rinehart, 1961.

Fisher, Dorothy C. "Vermont," *Holiday* Magazine. Philadelphia: November 1949.

Hill, Ralph N. *Contrary Country*. New York: Rinehart, 1961.

Hoyt, Murray. "Retirement of Oscar Matthews," *Vermont Life* Magazine. Montpelier: Autumn 1958.

Lewis, Sinclair. In *The Rutland Daily Herald*. Rutland: Sept. 24, 1929.

Newton, Earle W. *The Vermont Story*. Montpelier: Vt. Hist. Soc., 1949.

Ogden, Samuel R. *New England Vegetable Garden*. Woodstock: Countryman Press, 1957.

They Settled the Hills (pp. 53-56)

Allen, Ira. "Autobiography," *Ira Allen, Founder of Vermont, 1751-1814, Vol. I*, James B. Wilbur. Boston: Houghton Mifflin Co., 1928.

Dwight, Timothy. *Travels in New England and New York, Vol. II*. New Haven: Timothy Dwight, 1821.

Kalm, Peter. *Travels in North America, Vol. II*. London: T. Lowndes, 1772.

Thompson, Daniel P. "Description of the Town of Randolph," *The Vermont Historical Gazetteer, Vol. II*, p. 971. A. M. Hemenway, Burlington: 1871.

Escape to Vermont (pp. 77-80)

Chapin, Miriam. "Where are All Those Yankees?," *Harper's* Magazine. New York: December 1957.

DeVoto, Bernard. In *Harper's* Magazine. New York: May 1954.

Duffus, Robert L. *Williamstown Branch*. New York: W. W. Norton, 1958.

Johnson, Burges. "Vermont, the Non-conformed," *The Saturday Review*. New York: October 24, 1953.

Millstein, Gilbert. "Murmuring Pines and Martinis," *The New York Times Magazine*. New York: July 29, 1962.

Newton, Earle W. *The Vermont Story*. Montpelier: Vt. Hist. Soc., 1949.

Wakefield, Don. "Waiting for Reality; Death of a Small Town," *The Nation*, N.Y.: Sept. 20, 1965.

Autumn's Bright Harvest (pp. 89-92)

Buckingham, James S. *America, Historical, Statistic, and Descriptive, Vol. III*. London: Fisher, Son & Co., 1841.

Dwight, Timothy. *Travels in New England and New York, Vol. II*. New Haven: Timothy Dwight, 1821.

Godley, Joseph Robert. *Letters from America, Vol. II*. London: 1844.

Tyler, Royall. Letter in *Annals of Brattleboro*, compiled by Mary R. Cabot. Brattleboro: E. L. Hildreth & Co., 1921.

The Lost Art of Sneaking (pp. 101-104)

Hoyt, Murray. "Now in the Old Days," *Vermont Life* Magazine. Montpelier: Autumn 1963.

Time of the Leaf Watchers (pp. 113-116)

Aldridge, John W. Cited by R. L. Duffus in *The New York Times Magazine*. New York: March 13, 1955.

Burton, Hal. "Last Stand of the Yankees," *Saturday Evening Post*, Philadelphia: July 22, 1961.

Chapin, Miriam. "Where are All Those Yankees?," *Harper's* Magazine. New York: December 1957.

Fisher, Dorothy C. "Vermont," *Holiday* Magazine. Philadelphia: November 1949.

Galbraith, John Kenneth. "The Pleasures and Uses of Bankruptcy," *The Liberal Hour*. Boston: Houghton Mifflin Company, 1960.

Hill, Ralph N. *Yankee Kingdom*. New York: Harper, 1960.

Riesman, David. Cited in *Yankee Kingdom* (above).

Smith, William J. "My Poetic Career in Politics," *Harper's* Magazine. New York: January 1964.

White, William Allen. Cited in "Vermont", D. C. Fisher, *Holiday* Magazine. Philadelphia: November 1949.

Williamson, Chilton. Reviewing D. C. Fisher's *Vermont Tradition*. In *The Saturday Review*. New York: December 26, 1953.

Sufferings and Settlements (pp. 125-128)

Fairbanks, Edward T. "St. Johnsbury," *The Vermont Historical Gazetteer, Vol. I*, p. 395. A. M. Hemenway, Burlington: 1867.

Hall, Francis. *Travels in Canada and the United States in 1816 and 1817*. London: Strahan and Spottswoode, 1819.

Hubbell, Seth. *A Narrative of the Sufferings of Seth Hubbell in His Beginning A Settlement in the Town of Wolcott in the State of Vermont*. Danville: E. & W. Eaton, 1826.

Smith, Elias. *The Life, Conversion, Preaching, Travels, and Sufferings of Elias Smith*. Portsmouth, N.H.: Beck & Foster, 1816.

On Enjoying the Cold (pp. 137-140)

Greene, Anne Bosworth. *The Lone Winter*. New York: The Century Co., 1923.

Shall Her Mountains Die? (pp. 149-153)

Flanders, Ralph E. *Letters to a Generation*. Boston: Beacon Press, 1956.

Hill, Ralph N. *Yankee Kingdom*. New York: Harper, 1960.

Hoff, Philip H. In *Inaugural Message*. Montpelier: January 5, 1967.

Lee, W. Storrs. *The Green Mountains of Vermont*. New York: Holt, 1955.

Ogden, Samuel R. "VL Reports," *Vermont Life* Magazine. Montpelier: Spring 1968.

Skow, John. "The Sunday Afternoon Fox," *The Saturday Evening Post*. Philadelphia: December 5, 1964.

Stegner, Wallace. "The People Against the American Continent," *Vermont History*. Montpelier: Vt. Hist. Soc., Autumn 1967.

Index